AAT

Indirect Tax FA 2019
Level 3
Advanced Diploma in
Accounting
Course Book
For assessments from January
to December 2020

Fourth edition 2019

ISBN 9781 5097 2667 7
ISBN (for internal use only) 9781 5097 2664 6

British Library Cataloguing-in-Publication Data
A catalogue record for this book is available from the British Library

Published by

BPP Learning Media Ltd
BPP House, Aldine Place
142-144 Uxbridge Road
London W12 8AA

www.bpp.com/learningmedia

Printed in the United Kingdom

Your learning materials, published by BPP Learning Media Ltd, are printed on paper obtained from traceable sustainable sources.

BPP
LEARNING MEDIA

Contents

	Page
Introduction to the course	iv
Skills bank	vi
Chapter 1 Introduction to VAT	1
Chapter 2 VAT basics	9
Chapter 3 Inputs and outputs	23
Chapter 4 Accounting for VAT	41
Chapter 5 The VAT return	57
Chapter 6 VAT schemes for small businesses	83
Chapter 7 Administration	95
Activity answers	113
Test your learning: answers	125
Reference material	145
Index	181

Introduction to the course

Syllabus overview

This unit teaches students the knowledge and skills to calculate VAT and submit the VAT return. It involves extracting the relevant information from an organisation's accounting records; calculating the amount of VAT payable or reclaimable and resolving errors or omissions.

Students will also be able to submit completed documentation in a timely manner whilst maintaining an effective working relationship with the relevant tax authority.

Test specification for this unit assessment

Assessment method	Marking type	Duration of assessment
Computer based assessment	**Computer marked**	1.5 hours

Learning outcomes	Weighting
1 Understand and apply VAT legislation requirements	30%
2 Accurately complete VAT returns and submit them in a timely manner	40%
3 Understand the implications for the business of errors, omissions and late filing and payment	20%
4 Report VAT-related information within the organisation in accordance with regulatory and organisational requirement	10%
Total	**100%**

BPP
LEARNING MEDIA

Assessment structure

1½ hours duration

Competency is 70%

*Note that this is only a guideline as to what might come up. The format and content of each task may vary from what we have listed below.

Your assessment will consist of 8 tasks

Task	Expected content	Max marks	Chapter ref	Study complete
Task 1	Finding out about VAT, and registration	8	VAT basics, Accounting for VAT	
Task 2	VAT invoices, tax point, making exempt supplies	9	Accounting for VAT, Inputs and outputs	
Task 3	VAT schemes, due dates, bad debt relief	5	VAT schemes for small businesses, The VAT return	
Task 4	Detailed VAT rules, corrections, ethics	9	Accounting for VAT, Administration	
Task 5	VAT calculations and reconciliations	7	Inputs and outputs, The VAT return	
Task 6	Preparing specific figures for the VAT return, corrections, ethics	7	The VAT return, Administration	
Task 7	Completing and submitting a VAT return accurately	17	The VAT return	
Task 8	Communicating VAT information	8	Administration	

Skills bank

Our experience of preparing students for this type of assessment suggests that to obtain competency, you will need to develop a number of key skills.

What do I need to know to do well in the assessment?

Indirect Tax is designed to develop your skills in preparing and submitting returns to the relevant tax authority in situations where the transactions that have to be included are relatively routine.

To be successful in the assessment you need to:

*   Understand and apply VAT legislation requirements

*   Accurately complete VAT returns and submit them in a timely manner

*   Understand the implications for the business of errors, omissions, and late filing and payment

*   Report VAT-related information within the organisation in accordance with regulatory and organisational requirement

Assumed knowledge

There is no assumed knowledge for this unit.

Assessment style

In the assessment you will complete tasks by:

1   Entering narrative by selecting from drop down menus of narrative options known as **picklists**

2   Using **drag and drop** menus to enter narrative

3   Typing in numbers, known as **gapfill** entry

4   Entering **ticks**

5   Entering **dates** by selecting from a calendar

You must familiarise yourself with the style of the online questions and the AAT software before taking the assessment. As part of your revision, login to the **AAT website** and attempt their **online practice assessments**.

Introduction to the assessment

The question practice you do will prepare you for the format of tasks you will see in the *Indirect Tax* assessment. It is also useful to familiarise yourself with the introductory information you may be given at the start of the assessment. For example:

You have 1 hour and 30 minutes to complete this assessment.

You should attempt and aim to complete EVERY task.

Each task is independent. You will not need to refer to your answers to previous tasks.

Read every task carefully to make sure you understand what is required.

Where the date is relevant, it is given in the task data.

Both minus signs and brackets can be used to indicate negative numbers UNLESS task instructions state otherwise.

The standard rate of VAT is 20%

You must use a full stop to indicate a decimal point.

For example, write 100.57 NOT 100,57 OR 100 57.

You may use a comma to indicate a number in the thousands, but you don't have to. For example, 10000 and 10,000 are both OK.

Other indicators are not compatible with the computer-marked system.

Reference data is provided in this assessment. The data has been broken down into sections to make it easier to search. You can access the data at any point by clicking on the section subject listed in the toolbar at the top right of every task.

When you click on a subject, the data will appear in a pop-up window. You can then move or close the window. When you move on to a new task, you will have to re-open a window to see the data again.

---

1   As you revise, use the **BPP Passcards** to consolidate your knowledge. They are a pocket-sized revision tool, perfect for packing in that last-minute revision.

2   Attempt as many tasks as possible in the **Question Bank**. There are plenty of assessment-style tasks which are excellent preparation for the real assessment.

3   Always **check** through your own answers as you will in the real assessment, before looking at the solutions in the back of the Question Bank.

Key to icons

Key term — A key definition which is important to be aware of for the assessment

Formula to learn — A formula you will need to learn as it will not be provided in the assessment

Formula provided — A formula which is provided within the assessment and generally available as a pop-up on screen

Activity — An example which allows you to apply your knowledge to the technique covered in the Course Book. The solution is provided at the end of the chapter

Illustration — A worked example which can be used to review and see how an assessment question could be answered

Assessment focus point — A high priority point for the assessment

Open book reference — Where use of an open book will be allowed for the assessment

Real life examples — A practical real life scenario

AAT qualifications

The material in this book may support the following AAT qualifications:

AAT Advanced Diploma in Accounting Level 3 and AAT Advanced Diploma in Accounting at SCQF Level 6.

Supplements

From time to time we may need to publish supplementary materials to one of our titles. This can be for a variety of reasons, from a small change in the AAT unit guidance to new legislation coming into effect between editions.

You should check our supplements page regularly for anything that may affect your learning materials. All supplements are available free of charge on our supplements page on our website at:

www.bpp.com/learning-media/about/students

Improving material and removing errors

There is a constant need to update and enhance our study materials in line with both regulatory changes and new insights into the assessments.

From our team of authors BPP appoints a subject expert to update and improve these materials for each new edition.

Their updated draft is subsequently technically checked by another author and from time to time non-technically checked by a proof reader.

We are very keen to remove as many numerical errors and narrative typos as we can but given the volume of detailed information being changed in a short space of time we know that a few errors will sometimes get through our net.

We apologise in advance for any inconvenience that an error might cause. We continue to look for new ways to improve these study materials and would welcome your suggestions. Please feel free to contact our AAT Head of Programme at nisarahmed@bpp.com if you have any suggestions for us.

These learning materials are based on the qualification specification released by the AAT in April 2019.

Introduction to VAT

1

Learning outcomes

Having studied this chapter you will be able to:

1.2	**Explain the necessary interaction with the relevant tax authority**
	• Know that VAT is a tax on consumer spending, including knowing whether the tax falls on registered businesses or the end user
	• Know the relevant tax authority for VAT
2.2	**Calculate relevant input and output tax**
	• Know the difference between inputs and outputs, and between input tax and output tax

Assessment context

An awareness of how the VAT system works within the UK.

Includes important terminology which is used throughout the course.

Qualification and Business context

It is the responsibility of the business to collect VAT on behalf of HMRC. As an accountant, you should be aware of how this process works.

Chapter overview

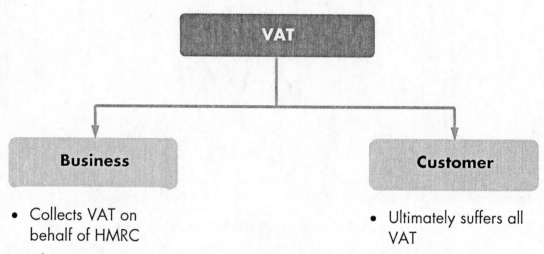

- **VAT**
  - **Business**
    - Collects VAT on behalf of HMRC
    - Charges output VAT to customers
    - Reclaims input VAT suffered on purchases
  - **Customer**
    - Ultimately suffers all VAT

Introduction

Value Added Tax (VAT) is an indirect tax which is essentially a sales tax – it is a tax on consumer expenditure and is an important source of revenue for the government. The basic principle is that VAT should normally be borne by the final consumer but is collected at each stage of the value added process.

Key term

> A VAT-registered trader will:
>
> **Output VAT** Collect VAT by charging their customers VAT
>
> **Input VAT** Reclaim VAT they have suffered on their purchases

A VAT-registered trader must complete a VAT return which states how much VAT is payable to Her Majesty's Revenue and Customs (HMRC). The amount payable is the difference between the output VAT and the input VAT. HMRC is the government department charged with the administration and collection of taxes.

The current rate of VAT is **20%**.

1 Role of a business

The business that is registered for VAT acts as an agent for HMRC, collecting VAT on their behalf. If the business adds value, it will owe output VAT to HMRC and that makes VAT a liability in the books of the business.

Businesses have to make sure they account for VAT accurately; otherwise they could face penalties.

2 Collection of VAT

It is the end consumer (normally the general public) who suffers the full amount of VAT. However, the VAT is collected by HMRC at each value added stage of the production process.

Illustration 1: Collection of VAT

	Net sale price £	Net purchase price £	VAT (@ 20%) £
Producer sells raw materials for £100.00 + VAT	100.00		20.00
Total payable by producer to HMRC			20.00
Factory buys the raw materials to manufacture their product. They then sell this product to a retailer for £300.00 + VAT		(100.00)	(20.00)
	300.00		60.00
Total payable by factory to HMRC	·		40.00
Retailer buys the product and sells it on to the end customer for £360.00 + VAT		(300.00)	(60.00)
	360.00		72.00
Total payable by retailer to HMRC			12.00

VAT paid to HMRC at each stage of the value added process is:	**£**
Producer	20.00
Factory	40.00
Retailer	12.00
Total	72.00
VAT suffered by end customer (who cannot reclaim) is:	72.00

Activity 1: Input and output tax

Business A sells goods to Business B for £1,000 plus £200 of VAT.

Required

Which business treats the VAT as input tax and which treats it as output tax?

	Input tax ✓	Output tax ✓
Business A		
Business B		

Chapter summary

- VAT is an indirect tax administered by HMRC.

- A purchaser who is not VAT-registered bears the cost of the VAT. This is normally the final purchaser in the supply chain, who is often a member of the public.

Keywords

- **Input VAT or input tax:** VAT on the purchases of goods and payment of expenses, which is reclaimed by the business from HMRC

- **Output VAT or output tax:** VAT on the sale of goods and the provision of services, which is paid by the business to HMRC

1   **Which organisation administers VAT in the UK? Tick the relevant box below.**

	✓
HM Customs & Excise	
Inland Revenue	
HM Revenue & Customs	
HM Treasury	

2   **Choose which ONE of the following statements is correct. Tick the relevant box below.**

	✓
Output VAT is the VAT charged by a supplier on the sales that are made by his business. Output VAT is collected by the supplier and paid over to HMRC.	
Output VAT is the VAT suffered by the purchaser of the goods which will be reclaimed from HMRC if the purchaser is VAT-registered.	

3   **Explain how it is normally the final consumer that pays the full amount of VAT to the seller but never pays any money to HMRC.**

VAT basics

Learning outcomes

Having studied this chapter you will be able to:

1.3	Describe the VAT registration and deregistration requirements
	• Registering for VAT
	• Registration and deregistration thresholds for the normal VAT scheme, and how to apply them
	• The circumstances in which voluntary registration may be beneficial to the business
	• The deregistration threshold and circumstances in which deregistration may be appropriate
	• What is meant by the past turnover measure and the future turnover method, and how to comply with them in respect of registration
2.2	Calculate relevant input and output tax
	• Recognise the different implications of exempt supplies and of zero-rated supplies for the VAT return, and the effect on recovery of input tax

Assessment context

Task 1 in the exam may ask you to identify when a taxable trader needs to register for VAT and also what the impact of this will be on the business.

Task 2 in the exam may ask you about exempt supplies and the difference between a zero-rated supplier and an exempt supplier. There is no knowledge required of the detail of which specific items fall into each category of supply.

Qualification context

Understand that not all businesses will need to be VAT-registered. However, if they are registered, you will need to know what the impact of this is.

Business context

You will need to have an awareness that there are different rates of VAT for different types of product.

The benefits of registering for VAT are abundant to a business, but consideration must be given to potential drawbacks.

Chapter overview

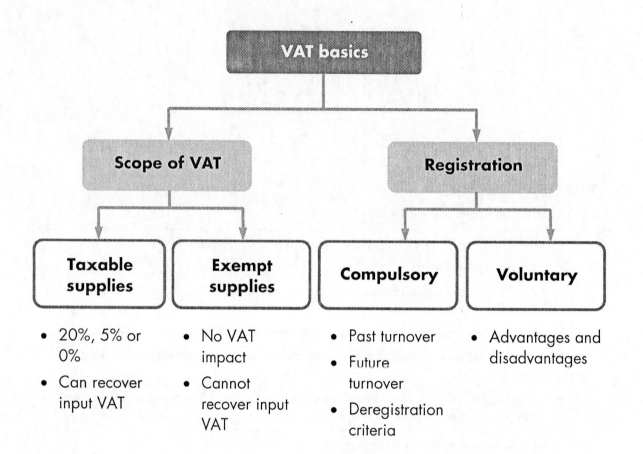

VAT basics

Scope of VAT

Registration

Taxable supplies	Exempt supplies	Compulsory	Voluntary

- 20%, 5% or 0%
- Can recover input VAT

- No VAT impact
- Cannot recover input VAT

- Past turnover
- Future turnover
- Deregistration criteria

- Advantages and disadvantages

1 Scope of VAT

VAT is chargeable on **taxable supplies** of goods and services made in the UK by **taxable persons** in the course of their business.

A **taxable person** is an individual or company who is required to register for VAT (see registration below).

Key term

> **Taxable supplies** are those which are:
>
> - **Standard-rated** (20%)
> - **Zero-rated** (0%) for example non-luxury food, children's clothing
> - **Reduced-rated** (5%) for example domestic fuel.
>
> **Exempt supplies** (eg, insurance or postal services) are not taxable supplies.

You will be told in the exam if a supply is taxable and, if so, at which rate.

A supplier making solely taxable supplies may, or in certain circumstances must, register for VAT and can then recover the input VAT suffered on their purchases.

If a supplier only makes exempt supplies, then they cannot register for VAT and will not be able to recover input VAT suffered on their purchases.

Illustration 1: Calculation of VAT payable

	Type of supplies		
	Standard-rated £	Zero-rated £	Exempt £
Supplies (net)	30,000	30,000	30,000
VAT charged on supplies	6,000	0	–
	36,000	30,000	30,000
Purchases (net)	20,000	20,000	20,000
VAT charged on purchases (all purchases are standard-rated)	4,000	4,000	4,000
	24,000	24,000	24,000
VAT payable/(reclaimable)	2,000	(4,000)	Nil

1.1 Cost to the business

- As businesses making taxable supplies that are registered for VAT can reclaim the input VAT paid on their purchases and expenses, the cost to the business is the VAT-exclusive amount.

- As businesses making only exempt supplies cannot register for VAT and therefore cannot reclaim the input VAT paid on their purchases and expenses, the cost to the business is the VAT-inclusive amount.

Activity 1: Cost to business

The following businesses have just paid telephone bills of £1,200 (£1,000 plus VAT of £200).

Required

What is the net cost incurred by each business in relation to the telephone bills?

Business type	Type of supply made	Net cost £
Insurance company	Only exempt supplies	
Accountancy firm	Only standard-rated supplies	
Bus company	Only zero-rated supplies	

2 Registration

2.1 Compulsory registration

Registration is compulsory if a taxable person meets one of the following two tests:

(a) Past turnover ('historic test')

Check at the end of each month if the total taxable turnover over the previous 12 months exceeds the registration limit of £85,000.

For a new business the period may be shorter, ie from the start of trade to the current month end. It must not, however, exceed 12 months.

(b) Future test

Each day check if the total taxable turnover over for just the next 30 days is likely to exceed the registration limit of £85,000.

Taxable turnover is the VAT-exclusive value of all zero-rated, reduced-rated and standard-rated supplies.

If either test is passed, the taxable person must notify HMRC within 30 days of the date of the historic test, and without delay for the future test.

Registration is effective from:

(a)   Start of month following the end of the 30-day notification period (historic test)

(b)   Start of the 30-day period (future test)

Illustration 2: Historic test

Jack started his business on 1 July 2019. His monthly VAT-exclusive turnover is:

	£
Standard-rated supplies	7,000
Zero-rated supplies	2,850
Exempt supplies	600
Total	10,450

1   Calculate the VAT-exclusive **taxable turnover** for each month (standard plus zero-rated supplies). Exclude the exempt supplies.

Taxable turnover is £9,850 per month (£7,000 + £2,850)

2   Work out when the £85,000 registration limit is exceeded (if at all), up to a maximum of a 12-month period.

After eight months (28 February 2020) cumulative turnover is £78,800, so the limit is not exceeded.

After nine months (31 March 2020) cumulative turnover is £88,650 so the limit is exceeded.

Therefore after nine months Jack must register for VAT within 30 days (ie by 30 April 2020). His registration will be effective from 1 May 2020.

Illustration 3: Future test

Orla has been in business for many years with VAT-exclusive turnover of approximately £6,500 per month (£78,000 per annum) and so has not yet had to register under the historic test. On 24 November 2019, Orla won a major contract which will immediately bring in additional income of approximately £78,800 per month.

Taxable turnover in the next 30 days alone will be £85,300 (£6,500 + £78,800), which exceeds the threshold, therefore Orla must register for VAT without delay, and her registration will be effective (ie she needs to charge VAT to her customers) immediately.

Activity 2: Mark – Registration

Mark commenced trading as a carpenter on 1 October 2019. He makes only taxable supplies. The turnover (net of VAT) for each quarter has been shown below. Turnover is spread evenly over the quarter.

Quarter ended	Turnover £
31 December 2019	18,000
31 March 2020	18,000
30 June 2020	22,800
30 September 2020	24,000
31 December 2020	25,500
31 March 2021	17,000

Required

(a) **When will Mark breach one of the registration tests?**

(b) **By what date is he required to notify HMRC that he is liable to register for VAT?**

(c) **When will Mark be registered for VAT?**

Solution

Activity 3: Registration scenarios

You have the following information about the taxable supplies of three businesses.

Required

For each of them, indicate whether they need to register for VAT immediately, or monitor turnover and register later. Tick ONE box on EACH line.

		Register now ✓	Monitor and register later ✓
A	A new business with an expected turnover of £8,000 per month for the next 12 months.		
B	An existing business with a total turnover of £79,000 for the last 11 months. Sales for the next 30 days are not yet known.		
C	An existing business with a total turnover of £7,500 per month for the last 12 months.		

Workings

2.2 Exemptions from compulsory registration

The registration requirement can be waived under two circumstances:

(a) If the business can satisfy HMRC that taxable supplies in the following 12-month period will be less than the deregistration threshold of £83,000.

(b) If the business makes only (or mainly) zero-rated supplies.

Registration decision tree

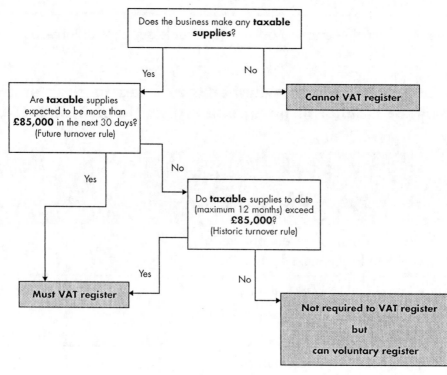

2.3 Voluntary registration

A business may apply for VAT registration even though its taxable turnover is below the registration threshold.

Zero-rated traders may choose to register early to produce a net repayment position.

2.4 Implications of registration

Some benefits and drawbacks of registration are highlighted below:

Advantages	Disadvantages
• Recover input VAT	• Administration burden
• Discipline	• Risk of penalties on errors
• Avoid late registration penalty	• Prices go up for non-VAT-registered customers as they cannot reclaim the input VAT on the purchase (need to look at customer status)

Activity 4: Voluntary registration

Choose ONE reason why a business making taxable supplies might choose not to register for VAT voluntarily.

		✓
A	Preparation of VAT returns would be required.	
B	Customers would benefit by being able to claim back input VAT.	
C	The business would benefit by being able to claim back input VAT.	

2.5 Deregistration

If the business ceases to make taxable supplies, it **must deregister**. The business must inform HMRC within 30 days of ceasing to make taxable supplies.

A business may **voluntarily** deregister if in the next 12-month period the VAT-exclusive value of taxable supplies will be below £83,000.

2.6 Failure to register

If the business fails to register on time, it will be taxed as if it had registered on time. The business will therefore still owe to HMRC the VAT that it should have been collecting on sales since the date on which registration should have been effective.

The business can calculate this in two ways:

(a) Treat its sales as VAT inclusive and pay the VAT out of profits.

(b) Treat its sales as VAT exclusive and try to get the extra money owed for the VAT from its customers.

Chapter summary

- There are two types of supply – taxable supplies and exempt supplies.

- In the UK there are three rates of VAT for taxable supplies – the standard rate of 20%, a reduced rate of 5% for certain supplies such as domestic fuel and power, and the zero rate.

- In a VAT-registered business, VAT does not increase the selling prices of either zero-rated supplies or exempt supplies. However, if a business makes exempt supplies, it cannot reclaim the input tax on its purchases and expenses. If the supplies made by the business are zero-rated, then input VAT can be reclaimed.

- The cost of purchases to a VAT-registered business making taxable supplies is generally the VAT-exclusive price. The cost of purchases to a business not registered for VAT, including a business making wholly exempt supplies, is the VAT-inclusive price.

- When a business's taxable turnover reaches the registration limit, the business must register for VAT; otherwise the business is liable for penalties (see Chapter 7).

- Some businesses may find it advantageous to register for VAT even though the registration limit has not been met – this is known as voluntary registration.

- If a business's taxable turnover falls below the deregistration limit, then the business can apply to HMRC to deregister.

- If a business ceases to make taxable supplies, then it must deregister.

Keywords

- **Exempt supplies:** Supplies on which no VAT is charged

- **Registration:** The process required if a business making taxable supplies must (if it exceeds the registration limits), or wants to, start charging (and recovering) VAT – VAT must be charged on taxable supplies from the date of registration

- **Standard-rated supplies:** Goods and services which are taxable at a rate of 20%

- **Taxable turnover:** This is the VAT-exclusive level of standard-rated, reduced-rated and zero-rated sales, but excludes exempt sales

- **Zero-rated supplies:** Goods and services which are taxable but the rate of tax on them is 0%

1 **Identify whether the following statements are true or false.**

	True ✓	False ✓
If a business supplies zero-rated services, then the business is not able to reclaim the VAT on its purchases and expenses from HMRC.		
A business makes zero-rated supplies. The cost to the business of its purchases and expenses is the VAT-exclusive amount.		

2 The following three businesses are trying to decide whether they need to register for VAT immediately, within the next 30 days, or whether they just need to monitor the situation for the time being.

Tick the correct box for each line.

	Register without delay ✓	Register within 30 days ✓	Monitor and register later ✓
An existing business with total turnover for the previous 11 months of £80,000. Sales for the next month are unknown at present.			
A new business with an expected turnover for the next 30 days of £90,000.			
An existing business with total turnover for the previous 12 months of £7,250 per month.			

3 You have been contacted by a potential new client, Mrs Quirke. She has recently started trading as an interior designer.

By selecting from the options listed, complete the following letter to her, explaining when her business must register for VAT.

AN Accountant
Number Street
London
SW11 8AB

Mrs Quirke
Alphabet Street
London
W12 6WM

Dear Mrs Quirke

VAT REGISTRATION

Further to our recent telephone conversation, set out below are the circumstances when you must register your business for VAT.

If the taxable turnover of your business at the end of a month, looking back no more than (1) [▾] months, has exceeded the registration limit of (2) [▾] , then the business must apply to register for VAT within 30 days.

Alternatively, if at any time the taxable turnover (before any VAT is added) is expected to exceed the registration limit within the next (3) [▾] alone, then the business must apply to be registered for VAT without delay. This would be the situation if, for example, you obtained a large additional contract for, say, £88,000.

If you wish to discuss this in any more detail, please do not hesitate to contact me.

Yours sincerely

AN Accountant

Picklists:

(1) 6   12   24
(2) £83,000   £85,000
(3) week   30 days   12 months

4. Amy started trading on 1 August 2018. Her monthly sales (excluding VAT) are:

	£
Standard-rated supplies	7,850
Zero-rated supplies	1,670
Exempt supplies	700
	10,220

By what date will Amy exceed the threshold for VAT?

By what date must Amy register for VAT?

5. Richard made taxable supplies of £74,500 in his first 11 months of trading. His taxable supplies in month 12 are £11,000.

Which of the following explains why Richard must register for VAT? Tick ONE box.

	✓
At the beginning of month 12, Richard expects his taxable supplies to exceed £85,000 in the next 30 days.	
At the end of month 12, Richard's taxable supplies in the previous 12 months will have exceeded £85,000.	

6. **Decide why a business making taxable supplies might choose to register for VAT voluntarily. Tick ONE box.**

	✓
Preparation of VAT returns would be optional.	
Customers would benefit by being able to claim back input VAT.	
Business would benefit by being able to claim back input VAT.	

Inputs and outputs

Learning outcomes

Having studied this chapter you will be able to:

2.2	Calculate relevant input and output tax
	• Calculate the VAT when given the net or gross amount of the supply
	• Know the specific calculations required for standard, reduced-rate, zero-rated and exempt supplies
	• Account for VAT on: expenditure on employee and business contact entertaining including that of mixed groups, purchases and sales of cars and vans
	• Understand the VAT rules on fuel scale charges, how to apply them and their effect on VAT payable or reclaimable
	• Understand how partial exemption works, the *de minimis* limit and how this affects the recovery of input tax
	• Calculate VAT for imports and acquisitions, exports and despatches
	• Identify the place of supply rules for both goods and services within and outside the EU
	• Understand how imports, acquisitions, despatches and exports are treated on a VAT return

Assessment context

Calculating and interpreting VAT is core to this unit. You will need to know how VAT is affected by different types of transactions. There is lots of information available in the reference material which will be available during the exam.

Task 5 will examine detailed VAT calculations.

Qualification context

You should be aware of the fact that the calculation of VAT changes depending on the type of transaction.

Business context

Every registered business needs to account for VAT accurately using the rules set out by the VAT legislation. These rules are some of the basics that you will need to be aware of in business.

Chapter overview

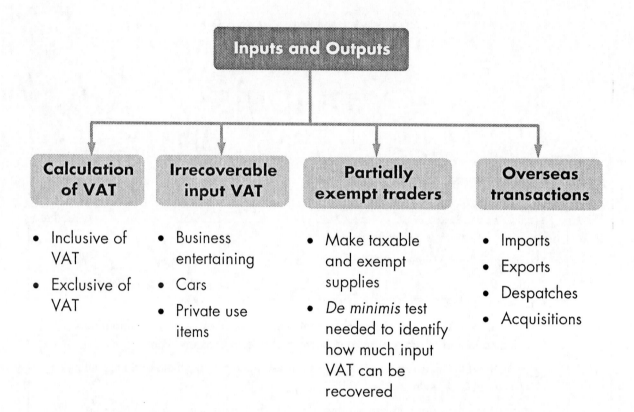

Inputs and Outputs

Calculation of VAT

- Inclusive of VAT
- Exclusive of VAT

Irrecoverable input VAT

- Business entertaining
- Cars
- Private use items

Partially exempt traders

- Make taxable and exempt supplies
- *De minimis* test needed to identify how much input VAT can be recovered

Overseas transactions

- Imports
- Exports
- Despatches
- Acquisitions

1 Calculating VAT

VAT charged on taxable supplies is based on the VAT-exclusive value.

Prices given to you by the examiner can be either inclusive (gross) or exclusive (net) of VAT. (You will always be told which is the case.)

Formula to learn

If an invoice shows that a standard-rated supply (VAT at 20%) has a **VAT-exclusive** amount of £100.00 then the VAT is calculated as:

£100.00 × 20% = £20.00

If an invoice shows that a standard-rated supply has a **VAT-inclusive** amount of £120.00, the amount of VAT can be calculated in one of two ways:

Either:

£120.00 × 20/120 = £20.00, or

£120.00 × 1/6 = £20.00

Type of supply	Apply to 'net' value (VAT exclusive)	Apply to 'gross' value (VAT inclusive)
Standard-rated supply	20%	1/6 (20/120)
Reduced-rated supply	5%	5/105

Illustration 1: Calculation of VAT

An invoice shows a total VAT-inclusive (gross) amount of £48.00. The amount of VAT at 20% included in this amount can be calculated as follows:

£48.00 × 20/120 = £8.00

or

£48.00 × 1/6 = £8.00

You can check this working by applying the 20% to the VAT-exclusive (net) amount:

£48.00 less £8.00 (VAT worked out above) = £40.00 (net amount)

£40.00 × 20% = £8.00

Activity 1: Calculation of VAT – Inclusive price

VAT-inclusive price = £642.00 (standard rate @ 20%).

Required

Calculate the VAT.

Solution

1.1 Rounding of VAT

Any VAT calculation should normally be rounded down to the nearest penny. (This concession is not available to retailers.)

Activity 2: Calculation of VAT – Rounding

An item has a net value of £54.89.

Required

How much VAT (@ 20%) should be charged on this item?

Solution

1.2 VAT payable to HMRC

Each VAT period (see Chapter 5) a taxable person will need to calculate how much VAT is owed to/repayable from HMRC.

This is calculated as:	£
Output VAT	X
Less:	
Input VAT	(X)
VAT payable/(repayable)	X/(X)

Activity 3: Calculation of VAT – VAT payable

A business buys goods for £1,000 excluding 20% VAT. It then sells those goods for £1,800 inclusive of 20% VAT.

Required

What is the total VAT paid to or reclaimed from the HMRC?

Choose one:

	✓
A £200 paid	
B £300 reclaimed	
C £100 paid	
D £100 reclaimed	

Solution

Usually (when input tax is recoverable), the cost to a VAT-registered business of buying goods and services is the **VAT-exclusive (net) amount**. For example:

	£
Amount paid to supplier (VAT inclusive)	1,200
Input VAT reclaimed from HMRC	(200)
Net cost to the business (VAT exclusive)	1,000

However, in certain circumstances, a business may not be able to recover all the input tax it has incurred on its purchases. Where VAT is irrecoverable, the cost to the business is the **VAT-inclusive amount.**

2 Irrecoverable input VAT

If a taxable person (one who is making taxable supplies – standard, reduced or zero-rated) is registered for VAT, then they will be able to recover their input VAT. There are, however, some circumstances where input VAT cannot be recovered.

2.1 Business entertaining

The input VAT incurred on business entertaining is not recoverable from HMRC. Business entertaining, however, does not include the following:

(a) Staff entertaining
(b) Entertaining of non-UK customers.

The recovery of input VAT, where there is a mixed group of staff and non-staff being entertained, would be apportioned appropriately.

2.2 Cars and vans

Unless a car is used exclusively for business purposes, then none of the input VAT, including the VAT on car accessories purchased at the same time, will be recoverable. (There will be no output VAT charged on disposal either as this will be an exempt supply.)

There are some exceptions to this, for example cars used:

*   Exclusively for business purposes (eg pool cars)
*   Within a taxi business
*   For driving instruction
*   Within a self-drive hire business

In the assessment, you will need to assume that the car has some private use unless told otherwise.

When purchasing a van, as long as the van is used at least partly to make taxable supplies, then the input VAT will be recoverable. For this reason, when the van is sold, output VAT would need to be charged on disposal.

Capital item	Input tax recoverable on purchase?	Output tax chargeable on sale of item?
New car for employee's use	NO	NO – Exempt
Car used in taxi business	YES	YES
Van	YES	YES

Activity 4: Reclaiming input tax

Identify whether input tax can be reclaimed by a VAT-registered business in each of the following circumstances.

Circumstance	Yes, can reclaim ✓	No, cannot reclaim ✓
Input tax incurred on entertaining prospective new UK client		
Input tax incurred on a new car for the top salesperson		
Input tax incurred on a car for use in a driving instruction business		

2.3 Private use

If an item purchased is being used for business and private purposes, then the portion of input VAT relating to the private use would not be recoverable.

2.4 Fuel for private use

Input tax on all road fuel purchased by the business and used for business purposes can be reclaimed.

However, when a taxable person purchases fuel and it is used for private motoring by an employee or the sole trader/partner, then this has an impact on the recoverability of the input VAT. The taxable person has a number of options:

(a) Ensure that the individual keeps sufficient mileage records so that the input VAT on just the business miles can be recovered.

(b) Reclaim all the input VAT suffered on fuel but then account for some **output VAT** using a set **fuel scale charge** per quarter. This scale charge is based on the CO_2 emissions of the vehicle, and will be given to you in the exam if needed.

(c) Agree not to reclaim any input VAT on fuel purchased for any (including commercial) vehicles.

Illustration 2: Fuel scale charge

Josie is an employee of SMH Ltd. She has the use of a car which is used for both business and private purposes during the current VAT quarter.

SMH Ltd pays all the petrol costs in respect of the car, totalling £1,200.00. SMH Ltd does not require Josie to keep accurate private mileage records. SMH Ltd wishes to reclaim the input VAT incurred.

The relevant quarterly fuel scale charge for Josie's car is £517.

All figures are inclusive of VAT.

The effect of the above on the quarterly VAT return is:

SMH Ltd may reclaim all of the input VAT on the fuel

£1,200.00 × 1/6 = £200.00

but must pay output VAT calculated on the fuel scale charge

£517.00 × 1/6 = £86.17 (note that normal mathematic rounding rules apply).

Activity 5: Reclaiming input tax on private fuel

Decide whether each of the following statements is true or false.

	True ✓	False ✓
A VAT-registered business can reclaim all the input VAT on road fuel if it keeps detailed records of business and private mileage, and makes no other adjustment.		
A VAT-registered business can reclaim all the input VAT on road fuel if it pays the appropriate fuel scale charge for private mileage.		

2.5 Partially exempt traders

How much input VAT a taxable person can reclaim is determined by the types of supplies they make, as discussed in Chapter 2 of this Course Book.

A taxable trader making only taxable supplies (standard, reduced or zero-rated) can reclaim all their input VAT, subject to the exceptions noted above.

An exempt trader, making only exempt supplies, cannot reclaim any of their input VAT.

There are, however, some traders who make both taxable and exempt supplies. These are called **partially exempt traders**.

Partially exempt traders:

(a) Only charge output VAT on their taxable supplies

(b) Can reclaim the input VAT on all purchases directly related to taxable supplies

(c) Can reclaim a proportion of input VAT which is not directly attributable to taxable or exempt supplies. This is based on the following calculation:

$$\text{Input VAT not directly attributable to taxable or exempt supplies} \times \left[\frac{\text{Value of taxable supplies made}}{\text{Total supplies made (taxable and exempt)}} \right]*$$

* round up to nearest per cent

The rest of the input VAT is only recoverable if it is below the **de minimis limit**: the amount is below £625 per month on average, **and** it is ≤ 50% of the total input tax for the period.

Assessment focus point

Note that your assessment will not test the detailed calculations. However, the following table should aid your understanding.

Input tax	Recoverable	Not recoverable
Directly attributed to taxable supplies	✓	
Directly attributed to exempt supplies		✗
Indirectly attributed (split using calculation)	✓	✗
	✓	✗ UNLESS below *de minimis* limits

Activity 6: Partially exempt trader – Calculation

For the quarter ended 30 June 20X9, Jim has allocated his input tax suffered between taxable and exempt supplies, but a balance remains unallocated.

Exempt £	Taxable £	Unallocated £	Total input tax £
700	20,000	3,000	23,700

His total turnover for the quarter was £135,429, of which taxable supplies amounted to £114,573.

Required

How much of the £23,700 input tax suffered is recoverable by Jim?

Attributable to taxable supplies

	£
Directly allocated	
Indirectly allocated:	

Attributable to exempt supplies

	£
Directly allocated	
Indirectly allocated:	

Activity 7: Partially exempt trader – Multiple choice

A business supplies goods that are a mixture of standard-rated, exempt and zero-rated.

Required

Which of the following statements is true? Choose ONE answer.

		✓
A	All of the input VAT can be reclaimed.	
B	None of the input VAT can be reclaimed.	
C	All of the input VAT can be reclaimed, providing certain (*de minimis*) conditions are met.	
D	Some of the input VAT can be reclaimed, in proportion to the different types of supply.	

3 Overseas Transactions

Please note these rules are, as yet, unchanged since the European Union (EU) referendum.

3.1 Determining the place of supply

UK VAT is charged on supplies within the UK. It is therefore important to understand whether or not a supply is 'in the UK'. This is determined by the 'place of supply' rules.

Goods are deemed to be supplied where they 'originate', or start their journey. If they are located in the UK before being shipped to a customer, the place of supply is the UK.

Services are a little more complex. If the supply is to a registered business customer (eg, the performance of a company audit by its external auditors), they are deemed to be supplied where the customer is located. Other supplies of services (to non-registered businesses or consumers) are deemed to be supplied in the seller's country.

3.2 Within EU

Supplies of goods to EU countries are referred to as **despatches** and are zero-rated if the trader obtains the customer's VAT number and can prove the goods left the UK. Otherwise, tax at the UK rate (ie 20%).

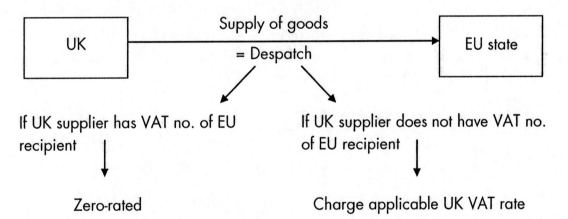

When goods are purchased from elsewhere in the EU, these are referred to as **acquisitions**; no VAT is charged by the supplier. The UK purchaser has to charge themselves output VAT on the VAT return. This is then offset by an equal amount of input VAT. For a fully taxable trader, the transaction is therefore VAT neutral.

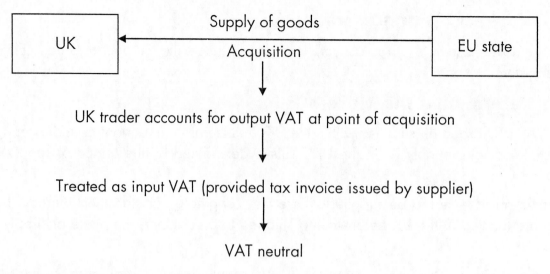

UK trader accounts for output VAT at point of acquisition

Treated as input VAT (provided tax invoice issued by supplier)

VAT neutral

Outside EU

If goods are supplied to countries outside of the EU, they are referred to as **exports** and are always zero-rated, provided the trader obtains evidence of their export within three months.

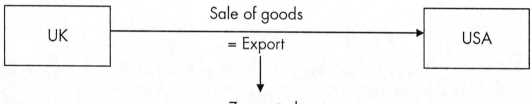

Goods which are purchased from countries outside of the EU are known as **imports**. No VAT is charged by the supplier. When the goods enter the UK, the purchaser needs to pay the applicable rate of UK VAT.

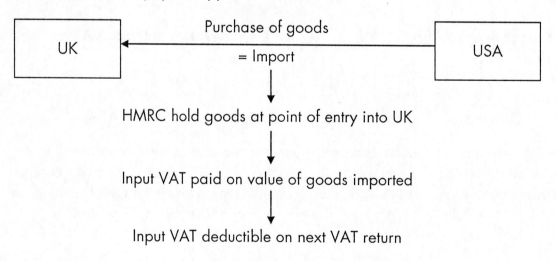

Activity 8: Despatches

A UK VAT-registered trader sells goods to both VAT-registered and non-VAT-registered traders elsewhere in the EU. If these goods had been sold in the UK, they would have been standard-rated.

Required

Which of the following is the correct treatment assuming all other conditions are fulfilled? Tick ONE box.

To VAT-registered traders	To non-VAT-registered traders	✓
Zero-rated	Zero-rated	
Standard-rated	Zero-rated	
Zero-rated	Standard-rated	
Standard-rated	Standard-rated	

Chapter summary

- VAT is charged on standard-rated supplies at 20%. The VAT amount in a VAT-inclusive price is found by multiplying by 1/6.

- The VAT on business entertainment expenses of UK customers and (usually) on the purchase of cars for use within a business is non-reclaimable.

- If input VAT is reclaimed on fuel used for private journeys, an amount of output VAT (the fuel scale charge) also has to be charged.

- If a VAT-registered business makes both taxable and exempt supplies, it is partially exempt. The recovery of input tax will be restricted, subject to the *de minimis* limits.

- Goods imported from outside the EU are charged at the same rate as goods in the UK. The tax is paid by the trader at the port or airport.

- The VAT on acquisitions of goods from other EU countries is treated as both output tax and input tax.

- Exports of goods to another country outside the EU are treated as zero-rated supplies.

- Despatches of goods to other EU countries are usually zero-rated if the customer is VAT-registered and has provided their VAT registration number. Otherwise, they are treated as if they were normal UK sales.

Keywords

- **Acquisitions:** Goods purchased from another EU country

- **Despatches:** Goods sold to another EU country

- **Exports:** Goods sold to a country outside the EU

- **Fuel scale charge:** An output VAT charge to offset against the input VAT reclaimed on fuel purchased for private use

- **Imports:** Goods purchased from a country outside the EU

- **Partially exempt traders:** When a business makes a mixture of taxable and exempt supplies, input VAT attributable to exempt supplies may only be reclaimed subject to satisfying *de minimis* tests

1   Business C sells goods to Business D for £384.00 plus the standard rate of VAT. Both businesses are VAT-registered.

    (a)   What amount of VAT will be charged on this transaction?

The VAT is	£	

    (b)   Which business will treat the VAT as output tax and which will treat it as input tax?

	Output tax ✓	Input tax ✓
Business C		
Business D		

2   **Identify which TWO of the following types of expenditure have irrecoverable input tax.**

	✓
Staff party	
Car for sales manager	
Photocopier	
Entertaining UK clients	

3   You have received four invoices from suppliers which show only the total VAT-inclusive price and the fact that all of the goods are standard-rated.

    For each invoice total, determine the amount of VAT that is included.

    Complete the following table.

VAT inclusive £	VAT at 20% £
42.88	
96.57	
28.20	
81.07	

4   A UK VAT-registered business is exporting goods which are standard-rated in the UK to a US-based business.

Which ONE of the following statements is correct? Tick the relevant box.

	✓
The goods will be treated as standard-rated in the UK if the US-based business is VAT-registered.	
The goods will be treated as standard-rated in the UK, provided documentary evidence of the export is obtained within three months.	
The goods will be treated as zero-rated in the UK if the US-based business is VAT-registered.	
The goods will be treated as zero-rated in the UK, provided documentary evidence of the export is obtained within three months.	

5   **Complete the following table.**

Net £	VAT rate %	VAT £	Gross £
	20		52.20
18.00	20		

6   **Decide whether each of the following statements is true or false.**

	True ✓	False ✓
A VAT-registered business can reclaim all the input VAT attributed to zero-rated supplies.		
A VAT-registered business can reclaim all the input VAT attributed to standard-rated supplies.		
A VAT-registered business can reclaim all the input VAT attributed to exempt supplies.		
A VAT-registered business can reclaim all the input VAT attributed to both taxable and exempt supplies, providing certain *de minimis* tests are satisfied.		

7   Joe, a VAT-registered trader, acquires goods from a VAT-registered supplier in another EU country.

Tick the box that describes how Joe should deal with this acquisition in terms of VAT.

	✓
No VAT is charged by the EU supplier; therefore this can be ignored by Joe on his VAT return.	
Joe must pay output VAT to HMRC at the port/airport and can reclaim input VAT on the next return.	
Joe must charge himself 'output VAT' and reclaim 'input VAT' on the same return.	

Accounting for VAT

Learning outcomes

Having studied this chapter you will be able to:

1.2	Explain the necessary interaction with the relevant tax authority
	• Explain the tax authority's rules about: what constitute VAT records; how long VAT records should be retained; how VAT records should be retained
1.4	**VAT invoices, required information and deadlines**
	• Know the correct contents and form of a VAT invoice, including the simplified VAT invoice rule
	• Determine the tax point of an invoice, both basic and actual, when the invoice is raised after the supply and also when there are: advance payments; deposits; continuous supplies; and goods on sale or return
	• The significance of the correct tax point for eligibility for special VAT schemes, applying the correct rate of VAT and determining the correct VAT for reporting
	• The time limits for issuing VAT invoices, including understanding the 14-day and 30-day rules
2.1	**Extract relevant data from the accounting records including:**
	• How to identify relevant accounting records that cover the required period of each VAT return
	• How to identify and extract relevant income, expenditure and VAT figures from the following ledgers and accounts: sales and sales returns, purchases and purchases returns; cash and petty cash accounts; and the VAT account
2.2	**Calculate relevant input and output tax**
	• Understand how to apply bad debt relief, when this is available and what time limits apply

Assessment context

You will need to be able to explain how different VAT transactions are treated, when they are accounted for and how the VAT payable to HMRC will be affected by each transaction.

Task 1 may include a question about VAT records.

Task 2 will involve questions about VAT invoices. This task may also involve a scenario in which you need to determine the tax point of a transaction.

Task 3 could look into bad debt relief, which is discussed at the end of this chapter.

Qualification context

This section of the notes will use your knowledge of a business's accounts. It is this information which will be used to produce the VAT return.

Business context

The accounting system within the business will need to store information which can be extracted in order to produce the VAT return. It is therefore important to know how the VAT transactions will be accounted for.

Chapter overview

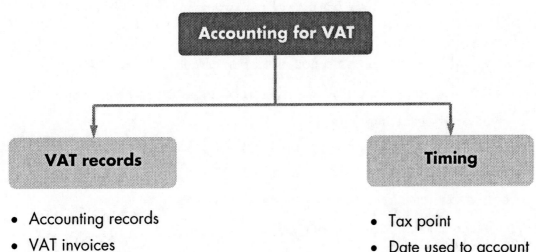

Accounting for VAT

VAT records

- Accounting records
- VAT invoices
- Simplified VAT invoices

Timing

- Tax point
- Date used to account for VAT
- Bad debt relief

1 Keeping records

1.1 VAT records

It is essential that businesses keep a record of all their transactions. Among other reasons, this is so that they are able to prove to HMRC that the level of input VAT which has been reclaimed is accurate. HMRC may also want to verify that the level of output VAT which has been paid has also been calculated correctly.

Generally the information that a VAT-registered business **must** keep includes:

- Business and accounting records

- Invoices issued and received in respect of transactions within the UK, acquisitions, despatches, imports and exports

- Credit/debit notes issued and received

- VAT account summarising output VAT and input VAT

The records which are kept should relate to both the **exempt and taxable** goods and services which the business has received and supplied.

The accounting records that most businesses keep in order to verify their sales include:

- **Sales day book** – this is a record of all of the invoices sent out to credit customers, showing the net amount of the sale, the VAT and the invoice total.

- **Sales returns day book** – this is a record of all of the credit notes sent out to credit customers, or debit notes received from credit customers, for returns and alterations to invoice amounts.

- **Cash receipts book** – this records receipts from credit customers as well as other receipts for cash sales.

- Orders and delivery notes, bank statements and paying-in slips.

The accounting records that most businesses keep in order to verify their purchases include:

- **Purchases day book** – this is a record of all of the invoices received from credit suppliers.

- **Purchases returns day book** – this is a record of all of the credit notes received by the business and any debit notes issued.

- **Cash and petty cash payments book** – this is a record of all of the cash payments made by the business.

All records need to be kept for a minimum of **six years**, and HMRC is entitled to inspect these records at any time. The supporting information for the VAT returns must be easy to find.

These lists of required records are in the reference material provided for you in the exam.

1.2 VAT invoice

VAT-registered businesses must raise a **VAT invoice** (paper or electronic) when they make a taxable supply to another VAT-registered business.

If the customer is not VAT-registered, then a VAT invoice is not mandatory, unless requested by the customer.

The invoice needs to be raised within 30 days of the supply. If an invoice is not raised, then the supplier has failed to keep proper records, and may have filed an incorrect VAT return, both of which carry potential penalties.

A taxable person can only reclaim input VAT if they have a valid VAT invoice for the purchase.

An example invoice is shown below:

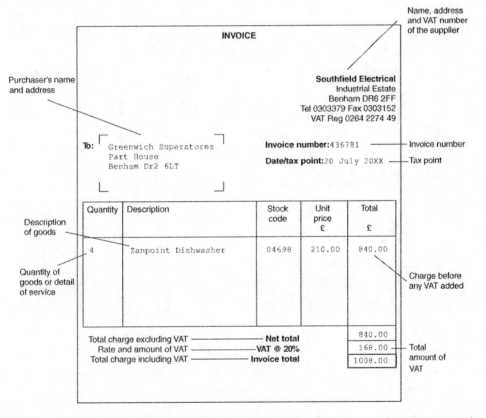

A VAT invoice must show all the information marked above. This list is included in the AAT reference material provided to you in the assessment.

Activity 1: Valid VAT invoice

Using your AAT reference material, which THREE of the following items must be included on a valid VAT invoice?

	✓
Customer VAT registration number	
Supplier VAT registration number	
Total VAT-exclusive amount for each type of item sold	
Total VAT amount charged	
Total VAT-inclusive amount for each type of item sold	

Processing a VAT invoice will have an effect on the VAT control account, and therefore will impact on the amount of VAT payable/reclaimable by the business. Purchase invoices and purchase returns will affect input tax, and sales invoices/sales returns will affect output tax.

Activity 2: Effect on VAT

A purchase invoice for taxable supplies has just been processed.

Required

What will be the effect on VAT? Choose ONE answer.

	✓
Input tax will increase	
Input tax will decrease	
Output tax will increase	
Output tax will decrease	

For **supplies invoiced at less than £250**, including VAT, a business may issue a less detailed **simplified invoice**. Suppliers do not need to keep copies of these simplified VAT invoices, although the customer would still need to keep the invoice if they wanted to reclaim the input VAT.

The reduced detail required on a simplified invoice is listed in the AAT reference material.

If the expenditure total is £25 or less including VAT, then no invoice is required to reclaim VAT for:

- Telephone calls or car park fees
- Purchases made through coin operated machines

1.3 Proforma invoice

A **proforma invoice** is often used in order to offer goods to a potential customer at a certain price and to invite the customer to send a payment, in return for which the goods will be despatched.

Businesses are not allowed to use this to reclaim input VAT, and, as such, any proforma invoice should be clearly marked 'THIS IS NOT A VAT INVOICE'.

If the customer does decide to buy the goods or sends payment, then a proper VAT invoice must be issued within 30 days of the supply or payment (if earlier).

Activity 3: Reclaiming input VAT

Decide whether the following statements are true or false. Tick the relevant boxes below.

	True ✓	False ✓
A 'simplified' invoice can be used to reclaim input VAT.		
A 'proforma' invoice can be used to reclaim input VAT.		

2 VAT and discounts

Many businesses offer discounts to their customers.

There are two types:

(a) **Trade discounts**

   (i) Given at the time of the sale/purchase, they reduce the selling price as an inducement to purchase.

   (ii) Usually for regular customers or **bulk buyers**.

(b) **Settlement discounts**

   If a supplier offers a settlement discount (a reduced price as an inducement to pay earlier than the normal credit terms), the VAT charged must be based on the actual consideration received. There are three ways of achieving this:

   (i) Issue the invoice based on the discounted amount, and a further invoice for the difference once the discount period has expired.

   (ii) Issue an invoice for the full amount, followed by a credit note if the discount is taken up.

(iii) Issue one invoice, with both possible prices and VAT amounts specified, with clear instructions to the customer regarding recoverability of their input VAT.

Activity 4: Settlement discounts

A business sells goods for £1,000 plus VAT, but allows a settlement discount of 5% for payment within ten days. The customer pays after eight days. The trader had decided to invoice for the full amount.

Required

What is the correct action for the trader?

	✓
Issue a further invoice for £50 plus VAT	
Issue a credit note for £50 plus VAT	
Take no action	
Issue a credit note for £50 including VAT	

Assessment focus point

VAT is calculated on the amount after trade discounts.

Remember to look for the actual amount the customer pays if you are asked for the amount of VAT on a transaction.

3 Credit notes and debit notes

Once issued, a VAT invoice cannot be amended. Amending an invoice can be viewed as an act of fraud.

Instead, additional documentation needs to be created if anything about the supply needs to be amended.

If the goods have been returned by the customer or the supplier has charged too much, then the supplier may raise a credit note to offset all or part of the original invoice (including the VAT element).

The credit note will decrease output VAT and will therefore reduce the amount payable to HMRC.

Alternatively, the customer could raise a debit note, which would have the same impact.

If too little was charged on the original invoice, a separate invoice should be raised for the difference.

Activity 5: Credit note

A business issues a credit note to a customer.

Required

Which of the following statements is correct for the business?

	✓
Input tax will increase.	
Input tax will decrease.	
Output tax will increase.	
Output tax will decrease.	

4 Tax point

It is possible that an order could be received, despatched, invoiced and payment made all in different quarters.

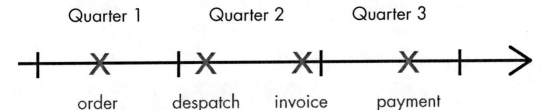

The **tax point** rules enable us to determine in which quarter to record the supply or purchase.

- The tax point is the earliest of the following events:

    - Despatch/goods made available/service completed (the **basic tax point**)

    - Invoice issued

    - Payment received

    (The order date is irrelevant.)

- If the basic tax point is the earliest date, then check if the invoice was issued within 14 days of that date. If it was, then the invoice date overrides the basic tax point and becomes the **actual tax point**.

Businesses may contact their VAT Business Centre and obtain their agreement in order to have the 14-day rule extended.

The following decision tree should help you to identify the relevant tax point of a transaction.

First, though, you need to identify the following three dates:

- BASIC TAX POINT (date of physical supply)
- Invoice date
- Payment date

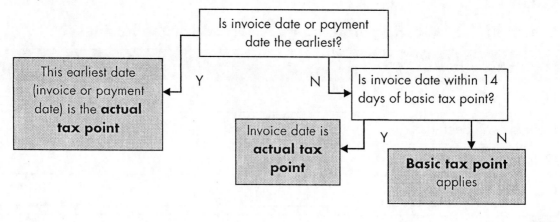

Activity 6: Alex – Tax point

Alex raises a proforma invoice and receives a payment in advance of making a supply. The proforma invoice was dated 18 May 20X2. The payment was received on 25 May 20X2. The goods were supplied on 29 May 20X2 and the VAT invoice was raised on 1 June 20X2.

Required

What is the tax point? Choose ONE answer.

		✓
A	18 May 20X2	
B	25 May 20X2	
C	29 May 20X2	
D	1 June 20X2	

Workings

If a deposit is paid separately from the balance, then two tax points must be identified.

Illustration 1: Tax point for deposits

On 1 August, a customer sent in a 15% deposit with an order. The goods were sent out to the customer on 6 August, and an invoice issued on 25 August. The customer paid the remaining 85% on 30 September.

The tax point for the deposit is determined by looking at:

- The basic tax point (delivery date)   6 August
- The invoice date   25 August
- The deposit payment date   1 August

The actual tax point is created at 1 August, as this is the earliest date.

The tax point for payment of the balance is determined by looking at:

- The basic tax point (delivery date)   6 August
- The invoice date   25 August
- The date of payment of the balance   30 September

The basic tax point is the earliest date. As the invoice date is more than 14 days after the basic tax point, the invoice date does not override it.

Tax point for the balance is 6 August (basic tax point).

Activity 7: Bang Ltd – Tax point

On 31 May 20X1, Bang Ltd ordered a new printing machine, and on 16 June 20X1 paid a deposit of £6,000. The machine was despatched to Bang Ltd on 30 June 20X1. On 18 July 20X1, an invoice was issued to Bang Ltd, showing the full amount and the balance due of £54,000. This was paid on 23 July 20X1.

Required

(a) **What is the tax point for the £6,000 deposit? Choose ONE answer.**

		✓
A	16 June 20X1	
B	18 July 20X1	
C	30 June 20X1	
D	23 July 20X1	

(b) **What is the tax point for the balance of £54,000? Choose ONE answer.**

		✓
A	16 June 20X1	
B	18 July 20X1	
C	30 June 20X1	
D	23 July 20X1	

Workings

5 VAT and bad debts

As a result of the tax point rules, output VAT is often paid over to HMRC before payment has been received from customers. If a debt subsequently goes bad, traders can reclaim VAT already accounted for.

All of the following conditions must be met for VAT **bad debt relief** to be available:

(a) The debt is over six months old (measured from when payment is due), and less than four and a half years old.

(b) The debt has been written off in the trader's books.

(c) The VAT must have been paid to HMRC.

The VAT being reclaimed on the bad debt is recorded as input VAT, rather than a reduction in output VAT.

These conditions are listed in the AAT reference material.

Activity 8: Bad debt relief

What effect will claiming VAT bad debt relief have on the amount of VAT due to HMRC? Choose ONE answer.

	✓
The amount payable will increase.	
The amount payable will decrease.	

Chapter summary

- All VAT-registered persons must keep full records of the details of all trade, both within the EU and outside the EU, and details of all standard-rated, reduced-rate, zero-rated and exempt goods and services, both purchased and sold.

- These records should normally be kept for six years and must be made available to an HMRC officer if required.

- Copies of sales invoices must be kept. The main accounting records for sales will be the sales day book, sales returns day book and the cash book.

- All invoices for purchases and expenses must be kept; otherwise the input VAT cannot be reclaimed. The main accounting records for purchases and expenses are the purchases day book, the purchases returns day book and the cash book.

- A VAT-registered business making a supply to another VAT-registered business must issue a valid VAT invoice within 30 days of making the supply.

- If goods are supplied for no more than £250, including VAT, a simplified (less detailed) VAT invoice can be issued which shows only the VAT-inclusive amount and the rate of VAT; however, if the customer asks for a full VAT invoice, this must be supplied.

- If a proforma invoice is sent out to a potential customer, this must be clearly marked 'THIS IS NOT A VAT INVOICE' as the customer cannot use it to reclaim any input VAT.

- The basic tax point is the date of physical supply. This basic tax point can be overridden by the actual tax point. The actual tax point can be created if an invoice is issued or a payment received before the basic tax point, or by sending out an invoice within 14 days of the basic tax point.

- If a business writes off a bad debt that is more than six months overdue and the output VAT on the supply has already been paid to HMRC, this VAT can be reclaimed from HMRC as input tax.

- **Actual tax point:** A further date that can override the basic tax point if certain conditions are met

- **Bad debt relief:** A reclaim of output VAT when a written-off debt is more than six months overdue

- **Basic tax point:** The date on which goods are delivered or services provided

- **Cash and petty cash payments book:** A record of all cash payments made by the business

- **Cash receipts book:** A record of all cash receipts of the business

- **Proforma invoice:** Often used to offer goods to potential customers; it is not a valid VAT invoice

- **Purchases day book:** A record of all invoices received from credit suppliers

- **Purchases returns day book:** A record of all credit notes received from credit suppliers

- **Sales day book:** A record of all invoices sent to credit customers

- **Sales returns day book:** A record of all credit notes sent to credit customers

- **Simplified invoice:** An invoice that can be issued if the VAT-inclusive value of goods supplied is no more than £250

- **Tax point:** The date which determines when the VAT must be accounted for to HMRC

- **VAT invoice:** A document that allows input VAT to be claimed or output VAT to be charged

Test your learning

1 **How long does HMRC usually require relevant VAT documents to be kept? Tick the relevant box below.**

	✓
1 year	
2 years	
6 years	
20 years	

2 **Which TWO of the following statements about proforma invoices are correct? Tick the relevant boxes below.**

	✓
A proforma invoice is always sent out when goods are sent to customers, before issuing the proper invoice.	
A proforma invoice should always include the words 'This is not a VAT invoice'.	
A customer can reclaim VAT stated on a proforma invoice.	
A proforma invoice is sent out to offer a customer the chance to purchase the goods detailed.	

3 **In each of the following situations, state the tax point and whether this is a basic tax point or an actual tax point (B or A).**

	Date	Basic (B)/ Actual (A)
An invoice is sent out to a customer for goods on 22 June 20X0 and the goods are despatched on 29 June 20X0.		
Goods are sent out to a customer on 18 June 20X0 and this is followed by an invoice on 23 June 20X0.		
A customer pays in full for goods on 27 June 20X0 and they are then delivered to the customer on 2 July 20X0.		

4   A VAT-registered business sends goods out to a customer on 15 May 20X0. The VAT invoice is then sent later and is dated 20 May 20X0. The customer paid the invoice on 20 June 20X0.

What is the tax point for these goods?

	✓
15 May 20X0	
20 May 20X0	
20 June 20X0	

5   A VAT-registered business received an order with a 10% deposit from a customer on 2 June 20X0. The goods were sent out to the customer on 11 June 20X0. The VAT invoice for the full amount is dated 29 June 20X0. The customer paid the remaining 90% on 31 July 20X0.

Identify ONE or TWO tax point(s) for these goods.

	✓
2 June 20X0	
11 June 20X0	
29 June 20X0	
31 July 20X0	

6   **State the conditions for the VAT on an irrecoverable (bad) debt to be reclaimed from HMRC.**

The VAT return

Learning outcomes

Having studied this chapter you will be able to:

2.3	Calculate the VAT due to, or from, the relevant tax authority
	• Disallow VAT that is not recoverable
2.5	Complete and submit a VAT return and make any associated payment within the statutory limits

Assessment context

Task 6 of the exam will require you to calculate the amount of VAT which will be included in a number of boxes of the VAT return.

Task 7 of the exam will require you to complete a full VAT return using data extracted from the accounting records. Additional transactions may need to be considered as well.

Qualification context

As a qualified accounting technician, you should be able to understand the impact that certain transactions have on VAT as a whole, as well as the VAT return.

Business context

Every registered business in the UK must generate a VAT return using the records which have been produced as part of the normal workings of the business. Most businesses will submit VAT returns via 'Making Tax Digital' software.

Chapter overview

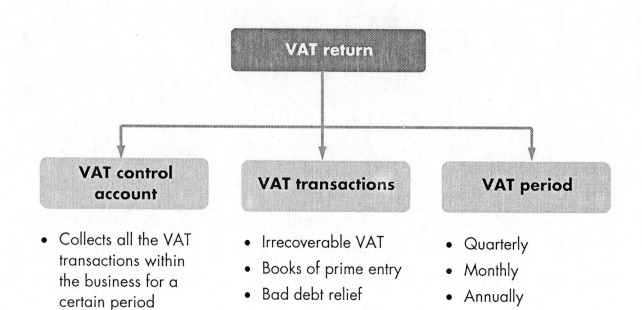

VAT return

VAT control account

- Collects all the VAT transactions within the business for a certain period

VAT transactions

- Irrecoverable VAT
- Books of prime entry
- Bad debt relief

VAT period

- Quarterly
- Monthly
- Annually

1 The VAT control account

As businesses collect VAT on behalf of HMRC, all VAT must be accounted for separately to the business's funds. This is done by maintaining a **VAT control account**.

VAT is normally owed to HMRC and so is usually a liability to the business. Credit entries into this account will increase the amount owed to HMRC, and debit entries will reduce the amount owed.

An example of the entries found in the VAT control account is shown below.

VAT control account

VAT deductible (input tax)	£	VAT payable (output tax)	£
VAT on purchases – from the purchases day book	3,578.90	VAT on sales – from the sales day book	5,368.70
VAT on purchases – from the cash payments book	586.73	VAT on sales – from the cash receipts book	884.56
	4,165.63		6,253.26
VAT allowable on EU acquisitions	211.78	VAT due on EU acquisitions	211.78
		Net understatement of output VAT on previous returns	287.52
Bad debt relief	33.60	Net overclaim of input VAT from previous returns	104.56
		Fuel scale charge	28.15
VAT on credit notes to customers – sales returns day book	69.80	VAT on credit notes from suppliers – purchases returns day book	49.70
Total tax deductible	**4,480.81**	**Total tax payable**	**6,934.97**
		Less total tax deductible	**4,480.81**
		Payable to HMRC	**2,454.16**

These double entries will have a direct link to the **VAT return** and therefore to the overall amount payable to/repayable by HMRC in the VAT period.

In the assessment, you will need to identify the impact that certain transactions have on VAT or specifically on the VAT account. Remember, purchase invoices and purchase returns (debit notes, or credit notes received **from** suppliers) affect input tax, whereas sales invoices and sales returns (credit notes issued **to** customers) will affect output tax.

Activity 1: Credit note – Impact on VAT

A credit note for taxable supplies is being processed.

Required

What will the effect on VAT be?

Choose ONE answer.

		✓
A	Input VAT will increase.	
B	Input VAT will decrease.	
C	Output VAT will increase.	
D	Output VAT will decrease.	

Workings

1.1 Impacts on the VAT account

Irrecoverable VAT

We know that businesses will be unable to reclaim input VAT on certain purchases and expenses. In this case, the VAT is part of the cost to the business and is therefore charged to the statement of profit or loss, or included in the cost of an asset on the statement of financial position.

For example, the double entry for buying a car for £10,000 (exclusive of VAT), where the VAT of £2,000 is irrecoverable, would be:

DEBIT   Motor vehicles account   £12,000
CREDIT   Cash account   £12,000

Activity 2: Irrecoverable VAT – Impact on accounts

You have the following extract from a manufacturing business's cash payments during the last month.

Required

Select either Yes or No in the right-hand box to show whether the input VAT can be reclaimed on the next VAT return.

Description	Net £	VAT £	Total £	Reclaim input VAT?
Office supplies	200.00	40.00	240.00	**Yes/No**
Purchase of company car	19,250.00	3,850.00	23,100.00	**Yes/No**
Computer	550.00	110.00	660.00	**Yes/No**
UK business entertainment	1,000.00	200.00	1,200.00	**Yes/No**

1.2 Bad debt relief

When a business recovers the output VAT from a bad debt, this will impact the VAT account.

For example, the double entry for a standard-rated taxable supply of £5,000 (exclusive of VAT) which has become a bad debt is as follows:

To record the initial sale:

DEBIT	Trade receivables	£6,000
CREDIT	Sales	£5,000
CREDIT	VAT account	£1,000 – the business expects to collect the VAT from the customer and therefore records it as VAT owed to HMRC

To record the bad debt:

DEBIT	Bad debt expense	£6,000
CREDIT	Trade receivables	£6,000

To reclaim the VAT on the bad debt (after the conditions have been met):

DEBIT	VAT account	£1,000 – the business needs to get that VAT back, and therefore reduces the VAT owed to HMRC
CREDIT	Bad debt expense	£1,000

1.3 Books of prime entry

The VAT account is part of the accounting system. As such, the books of prime entry will be used to post journals to the VAT account.

Activity 3: Books of prime entry – Impact on VAT account

Given below are some VAT figures taken from a business's books of prime entry.

Required

Identify whether the entry in the VAT control account will be a debit or credit. Tick the relevant box.

	Debit ✓	Credit ✓	£
VAT figures			
From the sales day book			8,750.00
From the sales returns day book			437.50
From the purchases day book			5,250.00
From the purchases returns day book			393.75
From the cash receipts book			1,514.45
From the cash payments book			837.55

2 VAT period

A VAT period is the length of time covered by each VAT return.

Most businesses have three-month VAT periods and submit quarterly returns in line with their year end.

However, there are some alternatives:

(a)   A business may be eligible for the annual accounting scheme (see Chapter 6) whereby only one return per year needs to be submitted.

(b)   Repayment traders (those who sell wholly or primarily zero-rated goods, so will be in a VAT repayment position) can apply to complete a monthly VAT return.

3 Clearing the VAT account

Illustration 1: VAT account entries

In the following example, a trader has output tax due to HMRC from quarter one of £2,500. The trader pays this to clear the account before the entries for quarter two are added.

In quarter two, total output tax on sales is £3,550 and total input tax on purchases is £1,750. This results in a balance due to HMRC of £1,800.

These total amounts will be shown on the VAT return for quarter two, with the balance of £1,800 being shown as VAT payable.

VAT account

Date 20XX	Reference	Debit £	Date 20XX	Reference	Credit £
QTR 1	VAT paid	2,500.00	QTR 1	VAT payable	2,500.00
QTR 2	Input tax on purchases	1,750.00	QTR 2	Output tax on sales	3,550.00
	Balance c/d	1,800.00			
	Total	**6,050.00**		**Total**	**6,050.00**
			QTR 2	VAT payable	1,800.00

Activity 4: Correction of error

A trader has VAT payable to HMRC for the quarter ended 31.03.20X0 of £3,750 and VAT payable for the quarter ended 30.06.20X0 of £4,200. These are the correct amounts shown on the VAT returns.

The trader pays the VAT for the quarter ended 31.03.20X0, but enters it onto the wrong side of the VAT control account.

Required

Identify the balance showing on the VAT control account before this error is adjusted.

	✓
£7,950	
£11,700	

4 The VAT return

4.1 VAT return

The boxes on a VAT return which a trader must fill in are as follows:

Box 1   **VAT due in this period on sales and other outputs:**

- The total of the output VAT on sales (include credit and cash sales)
- Less the VAT on any credit notes issued
- Plus any fuel scale charges
- Plus adjustments for earlier period errors (see Chapter 7).

Box 2   The **VAT due on any acquisitions** from other EU countries.

Box 3   The total of boxes 1 and 2.

Box 4   **VAT reclaimed in this period on purchases and other inputs, including acquisitions from the EC:**

- The total of the input VAT on purchases and expenses (include credit and cash purchases)

- Less the VAT on any credit notes received

- Plus the VAT on any acquisitions from other EU countries

- Plus bad debt relief

- Plus adjustments for earlier period errors (see Chapter 7).

Box 5   **Net VAT to be paid to HM Revenue & Customs or reclaimed by you:**

- Deduct box 4 (input tax) from box 3 (output tax)

- If box 3 (output tax) > box 4 (input tax), then tax is payable to HMRC

- If box 4 (input tax) > box 3 (output tax), then tax is reclaimable from HMRC

Boxes 6–9 deal with sales and purchases before any VAT is added. Accounting records such as purchases day books, sales day books and journals will be needed to complete these figures. Note that boxes 6–9 are stated in whole pounds (ie no pence are needed).

Box 6 **Total value of sales and all other outputs, excluding any VAT:**

This is the total of all sales, **less credit notes issued**, excluding VAT. It includes:

- Standard-rated sales
- Zero-rated sales (including exports)
- Exempt sales
- Supplies to EU member countries (despatches)

Box 7 **Total value of purchases and all other inputs, excluding any VAT:**

This is the total of all purchases and other expenses, **less credit notes received**, excluding VAT. It includes:

- Standard-rated supplies (including standard-rated imports)
- Zero-rated supplies (including zero-rated imports)
- Exempt supplies
- Acquisitions from EU member countries

Box 8 **Total value of all supplies of goods and related costs, excluding any VAT, to other EC Member States:**

Note. This figure is also included in box 6.

For the purposes of this assessment, you should not include in box 8 the value of goods supplied to EU customers who are not VAT-registered.

Box 9 **Total value of all acquisitions of goods and related costs, excluding any VAT, from other EC Member States:**

Note. This figure is also included in box 7.

(Related costs includes items such as freight costs and insurance for the goods.)

The **value** of the supply or acquisition of goods from other EU countries is shown on the VAT return separately. This is used to provide information on movements of taxable goods within the EU.

These details are provided in the AAT reference material available during the assessment.

Below is a copy of the format of the VAT return that you can expect to see in the computer-based assessment.

VAT return for quarter ended		£
VAT due in this period on **sales** and other outputs	Box 1	
VAT due in this period on **acquisitions** from other **EC Member States**	Box 2	
Total VAT due (**the sum of boxes 1 and 2**)	Box 3	
VAT reclaimed in this period on **purchases** and other inputs, including acquisitions from the EC	Box 4	
Net VAT to be paid to HM Revenue & Customs or reclaimed by you (**difference between boxes 3 and 4 – if box 4 is greater than box 3, use a minus sign**)	Box 5	
Total value of **sales** and all other outputs excluding any VAT. **Include your box 8 figure. Whole pounds only**	Box 6	
Total value of **purchases** and all other inputs excluding any VAT. **Include your box 9 figure. Whole pounds only**	Box 7	
Total value of all **supplies** of goods and related costs, excluding any VAT, to other **EC Member States. Whole pounds only**	Box 8	
Total value of all **acquisitions** of goods and related costs, excluding any VAT, from other **EC Member States. Whole pounds only**	Box 9	

Information for boxes 1–4 can usually be extracted from the VAT account.

Illustration 2: Completing the VAT return

This illustration shows how the business and accounting records are likely to be presented to you in the assessment.

The relevant ledger accounts are shown below for the quarter ended 31.03.20XX.

Sales and sales returns account

Date 20XX	Reference	Debit £	Date 20XX	Reference	Credit £
1.1–31.3	Sales returns day book – UK sales	2,374.00	1.1–31.3	Sales day book – UK sales	52,111.00
			1.1–31.3	Sales day book – EU despatches	9,700.00
			1.1–31.3	Sales day book – exports	4,259.00
31.3	Balance c/d	74,041.00	1.1–31.3	Cash book – UK sales	10,345.00
	Total	**76,415.00**		**Total**	**76,415.00**

Purchases and purchases returns account

Date 20XX	Reference	Debit £	Date 20XX	Reference	Credit £
1.1–31.3	Purchases day book – UK purchases	17,980.00	1.1–31.3	Purchases returns day book – UK purchases	1,020.00
1.1–31.3	Purchases day book – EU acquisitions	3,256.00			
1.1–31.3	Purchases day book – zero-rated imports	2,220.00	31.3	Balance c/d	22,436.00
	Total	**23,456.00**		**Total**	**23,456.00**

VAT account

Date 20XX	Reference	Debit £	Date 20XX	Reference	Credit £
1.1–31.3	Sales returns day book	474.80	1.1–31.3	Sales day book	10,422.20
1.1–31.3	Purchases day book	3,596.00	1.1–31.3	Cash book – UK sales	2,069.00
			1.1–31.3	Purchases returns day book – UK purchases	204.00

The following journal entry has been made to reflect a bad debt that is to be recoverable this quarter.

	Debit £	Credit £
Bad debts expense account (net amount)	975.00	
VAT account	195.00	
Sales ledger control account (gross amount)		1,170.00

In addition, you are told that a fuel scale charge of £28.83 applies for the private use of an employee's car and VAT on EU acquisitions is £651.20.

EU despatches are to VAT-registered customers.

5 How to complete the VAT return

Now to complete the boxes. Note that figures are shown in pounds and pence in boxes 1–5, with the figures being rounded down (if necessary) to pounds for boxes 6–9.

Workings

		£
Box 1	VAT on sales from the sales day book	10,422.20
	VAT on sales from the cash book	2,069.00
	Fuel scale charge	28.83
	Less VAT on credit notes	(474.80)
		12,045.23

		£
Box 2	VAT due on EU acquisitions	651.20
Box 3	Total of box 1 and box 2 £12,045.23 + £651.20	12,696.43
Box 4	VAT on purchases from purchases day book	3,596.00
	VAT on EU acquisitions	651.20
	Bad debt relief	195.00
	Less VAT on credit notes from suppliers	(204.00)
		4,238.20
Box 5	Net VAT due box 3 minus box 4	
	£12,696.43 – £4,238.20	8,458.23
Box 6	Standard-rated credit UK sales	52,111.00
	Less standard-rated credit notes	(2,374.00)
	Cash sales	10,345.00
	EU despatches	9,700.00
	Exports	4,259.00
		74,041
Box 7	Standard-rated credit purchases	17,980.00
	Less standard-rated credit notes	(1,020.00)
	EU acquisitions	3,256.00
	Imports	2,220.00
		22,436
Box 8	EU sales	9,700
Box 9	EU acquisitions	3,256

VAT return for quarter ended 31.03.20XX		£
VAT due in this period on **sales** and other outputs	Box 1	12,045.23
VAT due in this period on **acquisitions** from other **EC Member States**	Box 2	651.20
Total VAT due (**the sum of boxes 1 and 2**)	Box 3	12,696.43

VAT return for quarter ended 31.03.20XX		£
VAT reclaimed in this period on **purchases** and other inputs, including acquisitions from the EC	Box 4	4,238.20
Net VAT to be paid to HM Revenue & Customs or reclaimed by you (**difference between boxes 3 and 4 – if box 4 is greater than box 3, use a minus sign**)	Box 5	8,458.23
Total value of **sales** and all other outputs excluding any VAT. **Include your box 8 figure. Whole pounds only**	Box 6	74,041
Total value of **purchases** and all other inputs excluding any VAT. **Include your box 9 figure. Whole pounds only**	Box 7	22,436
Total value of all **supplies** of goods and related costs, excluding any VAT, to other **EC Member States. Whole pounds only**	Box 8	9,700
Total value of all **acquisitions** of goods and related costs, excluding any VAT, from other **EC Member States. Whole pounds only**	Box 9	3,256

Activity 5: David Ltd – VAT return

VAT exercise

The following details have been extracted from the daybooks of David Ltd.

Sales: UK

Date		Debit £	Credit £
31/10/X2	Sales day book		20,629.77
30/11/X2	Sales day book		23,673.85
31/12/X2	Sales day book		25,497.42

Sales: EU despatches

Date		Debit £	Credit £
31/10/X2	Sales day book		2,292.10
30/11/X2	Sales day book		2,406.72
31/12/X2	Sales day book		2,502.99

Purchases: UK

Date		Debit £	Credit £
31/10/X2	Purchases day book	14,231.10	
30/11/X2	Purchases day book	15,962.63	
31/12/X2	Purchases day book	16,436.91	

VAT: output tax

Date		Debit £	Credit £
31/10/X2	Sales day book		4,125.95
30/11/X2	Sales day book		4,734.77
31/12/X2	Sales day book		5,099.84

VAT: input tax

Date		Debit £	Credit £
31/10/X2	Purchases day book	2,846.22	
30/11/X2	Purchases day book	3,192.52	
31/12/X2	Purchases day book	3,287.38	

- Bad debt relief on a sales invoice for £85.41 including VAT is to be claimed in this quarter.
- VAT returns are completed online quarterly.
- VAT payable or receivable is settled by electronic bank transfer.
- In addition to the above purchases, the company acquired goods with a value of £4,500 from a French supplier on 14/12/X2.
- Today's date is 15/01/X3.

Required

(a) **Calculate and insert the figure to be reclaimed for bad debt relief.**

£	

(b) Complete boxes 1 to 9 of the VAT return for the quarter ended 31 December X2.

		£
Box 1	VAT due in this period on **sales** and other outputs	
Box 2	VAT due in this period on **acquisitions** from other **EC Member States**	
Box 3	Total VAT due (**the sum of boxes 1 and 2**)	
Box 4	VAT reclaimed in the period on **purchases** and other inputs, including acquisitions from the EC	
Box 5	Net VAT to be paid to HM Revenue & Customs or reclaimed by you (**difference between boxes 3 and 4**)	
Box 6	Total value of **sales** and all other outputs excluding any VAT. **Include your box 8 figure. Whole pounds only**	
Box 7	Total value of **purchases** and all other inputs excluding any VAT. **Include your box 9 figure. Whole pounds only**	
Box 8	Total value of all **supplies** of goods and related costs, excluding any VAT, to other **EC Member States. Whole pounds only**	
Box 9	Total value of all **acquisitions** of goods and related costs, excluding any VAT, from other **EC Member States. Whole pounds only**	

Working

5.1 Submission deadlines

It is mandatory for most VAT-registered traders to submit their returns online and pay electronically.

In this case, their submission and payment will be due seven calendar days after the end of the month following the end of the return period.

For example, the submission and payment date for the quarter ended 31 March will be 7 May.

The exceptions to this rule are as follows:

(a)   Traders who are eligible for the annual accounting scheme (see Chapter 6).

(b)   Traders who are still able to submit paper returns. For them, the submission date is one month after the end of the VAT period.

(c)   Traders who make payments on account (see Chapter 6). For them, the submission date is one month after the end of the VAT period.

(d)   Traders who pay by direct debit. These businesses will receive an extra three days on top of the normal submission date to make the payment.

This information is in the AAT reference material available in your assessment.

5.2 Making Tax Digital

For VAT periods starting on or after 1 April 2019, most VAT registered businesses with taxable turnover above the VAT registration threshold must use the Making Tax Digital (MTD) service to keep records and submit their VAT returns. They must then continue to use the MTD service even if their turnover falls below the registration threshold.

The only exceptions to this requirement are as follows:

*   If it is not reasonably practicable for the business to use digital tools, for example due to age, disability or remoteness

*   If the business is subject to an insolvency procedure

*   Or if the business is run by members of a religious society or order whose beliefs are not compatible with using computers

If a VAT registered business has taxable turnover below the VAT registration threshold they may choose to use MTD services, and can stop again should they so wish.

To ease the transition to MTD the HMRC are allowing a period of one year, to 1 April 2020, known as a "soft landing period", before businesses have to be able to join up all of their records with digital links.

This information is in the AAT reference material available in your assessment.

Chapter summary

- The VAT account records the VAT payable and reclaimable by the business and is a link between the business records and the VAT return.

- Normally every quarter the VAT return must be completed and submitted to HMRC, together with any payment, by the due date.

- The first five boxes of the VAT return can usually be completed from the figures in the VAT account.

- Boxes 6 to 9 must be completed from the other accounting records of the business showing sales, purchases, despatches and acquisitions, all excluding VAT.

- The VAT return is generally due one month and seven days following the end of the relevant VAT return period.

- For periods starting on or after 1 April 2019 most businesses have to use the Making Tax Digital service to keep records and submit VAT returns.

Keywords

- **VAT (control) account:** The ledger account in which all amounts of input tax and output tax are recorded

- **VAT return:** The form which must be completed and submitted to HMRC to show the amount of VAT due or to be reclaimed, usually for the quarter

- **Making Tax Digital:** The service most businesses must start to use to keep digital records and submit their VAT returns

- **Soft landing period:** The one year grace period allowed by the HMRC for the transition to ensuring all data within a business can be transferred digitally

1 **Decide whether the following statements are true or false. Tick the relevant boxes below.**

	True ✓	False ✓
If input VAT is greater than output VAT on the return, VAT is payable to HMRC.		
If output VAT is greater than input VAT on the return, VAT is repayable from HMRC.		

2 Holly completed her VAT return for the latest quarter. It correctly indicates that she owes HMRC £7,520 of VAT. However, her VAT account is showing an amount due of £12,220. VAT payable for the previous quarter was £4,700.

Tick which ONE of the following statements explains the difference.

	✓
The payment of £4,700 for the previous quarter has been included twice in the VAT account.	
The payment of £4,700 for the previous quarter has been omitted from the VAT account.	

3 The ledger accounts of a VAT-registered trader for the quarter ended 30.06.20XX are shown below:

Sales and sales returns account

Date 20XX	Reference	Debit £	Date 20XX	Reference	Credit £
1.4–30.6	Sales returns day book – UK sales	2,400.00	1.4–30.6	Sales day book – UK sales	26,000.00
			1.4–30.6	Sales day book – exports	5,800.00
30.6	Balance c/d	43,400.00	1.4–30.6	Cash book – UK sales	14,000.00
	Total	**45,800.00**		**Total**	**45,800.00**

Purchases account

Date 20XX	Reference	Debit £	Date 20XX	Reference	Credit £
1.4–30.6	Purchases day book – UK purchases	15,500.00			
1.4–30.6	Purchases day book – EU acquisitions	3,750.00	30.6	Balance c/d	19,250.00
	Total	**19,250.00**		**Total**	**19,250.00**

VAT account

Date 20XX	Reference	Debit £	Date 20XX	Reference	Credit £
1.4–30.6	Sales returns day book	480.00	1.4–30.6	Sales day book	5,200.00
1.4–30.6	Purchases day book	3,100.00	1.4–30.6	Cash book – UK sales	2,800.00

In addition, you are told that bad debt relief on a sales invoice of £500.00 excluding VAT is to be claimed this quarter.

VAT on EU acquisitions is £750.00.

Complete boxes 1 to 9 of the VAT return below for the quarter ended 30.06.20XX.

VAT return for quarter ended 30.06.20XX		£
VAT due in this period on **sales** and other outputs	Box 1	
VAT due in this period on **acquisitions** from other **EC Member States**	Box 2	
Total VAT due (**the sum of boxes 1 and 2**)	Box 3	
VAT reclaimed in this period on **purchases** and other inputs, including acquisitions from the EC	Box 4	

VAT return for quarter ended 30.06.20XX		£
Net VAT to be paid to HM Revenue & Customs or reclaimed by you (**difference between boxes 3 and 4 – if box 4 is greater than box 3, use a minus sign**)	Box 5	
Total value of **sales** and all other outputs, excluding any VAT. **Include your box 8 figure. Whole pounds only**	Box 6	
Total value of **purchases** and all other inputs, excluding any VAT. **Include your box 9 figure. Whole pounds only**	Box 7	
Total value of all **supplies** of goods and related costs, excluding any VAT, to other **EC Member States. Whole pounds only**	Box 8	
Total value of all **acquisitions** of goods and related costs, excluding any VAT, from other **EC Member States. Whole pounds only**	Box 9	

4   The ledger accounts shown below are those of a VAT-registered trader for the quarter ended 31 May 20XX.

Sales and sales returns account

Date 20XX	Reference	Debit £	Date 20XX	Reference	Credit £
1.3–31.5	Sales returns day book – UK standard-rated sales	398.86	1.3–31.5	Sales day book – UK standard-rated sales	30,678.25
1.3–31.5	Sales returns day book – UK zero-rated sales	25.59	1.3–31.5	Sales day book – UK zero-rated sales	3,581.67
31.5	Balance c/d	38,889.98	1.3–31.5	Cash book – UK standard-rated sales	5,054.51
	Total	**39,314.43**		**Total**	**39,314.43**

Purchases account

Date 20XX	Reference	Debit £	Date 20XX	Reference	Credit £
1.3–31.5	Purchases day book – UK standard-rated purchases	20,450.85			
1.3–31.5	Purchases day book – UK zero-rated purchases	2,669.80			
1.3–31.5	Cash book – UK standard-rated purchases/ expenses	3,033.01	31.5	Balance c/d	26,153.66
	Total	**26,153.66**		**Total**	**26,153.66**

VAT account

Date 20XX	Reference	Debit £	Date 20XX	Reference	Credit £
1.3–31.5	Sales returns day book	79.77	1.3–31.5	Sales day book	6,135.65
1.3–31.5	Purchases day book	4,090.17	1.3–31.5	Cash book	1,010.90
1.3–31.5	Cash book	606.60			

Journal (extract)

	Debit £	Credit £
Irrecoverable (bad) debts expense	192.00	
VAT account	38.40	
Receivables (debtors) (VAT inclusive at 20%)		230.40

Complete boxes 1 to 9 of the VAT return for the quarter ended 31 May 20XX.

VAT return for quarter ended 31.05.20XX		£
VAT due in this period on **sales** and other outputs	Box 1	
VAT due in this period on **acquisitions** from other **EC Member States**	Box 2	
Total VAT due **(the sum of boxes 1 and 2)**	Box 3	
VAT reclaimed in this period on **purchases** and other inputs, including acquisitions from the EC	Box 4	
Net VAT to be paid to HM Revenue & Customs or reclaimed by you **(difference between boxes 3 and 4 – if box 4 is greater than box 3, use a minus sign)**	Box 5	
Total value of **sales** and all other outputs excluding any VAT. **Include your box 8 figure. Whole pounds only**	Box 6	
Total value of **purchases** and all other inputs excluding any VAT. **Include your box 9 figure. Whole pounds only**	Box 7	
Total value of all **supplies** of goods and related costs, excluding any VAT, to other **EC Member States. Whole pounds only**	Box 8	
Total value of all **acquisitions** of goods and related costs, excluding any VAT, from other **EC Member States. Whole pounds only**	Box 9	

5 **Identify which ONE of the following statements in relation to acquisition of goods from other EU countries and how they are dealt with on the VAT return is correct.**

	✓
Input tax paid at the ports is reclaimed as input tax on the VAT return.	
Both input tax and output tax in relation to the goods are shown on the VAT return.	
They are zero-rated and so no VAT features on the VAT return.	
They are exempt and so no VAT features on the VAT return.	

6 **Identify which of the following statement(s) is/are correct. There may be more than one correct statement.**

	✓
The fuel scale charge increases output VAT and is shown in box 1.	
VAT on EU acquisitions increases both input VAT and output VAT and is shown in boxes 1 and 4.	
Credit notes received from suppliers reduce input VAT and are shown in box 4.	
Credit notes issued to customers reduce output VAT and are shown in box 1.	

7 Vincent is VAT-registered and sells standard-rated items both in the UK and overseas. Sales (excluding VAT) for the quarter ended 31.3.20X0 are split as follows:
   - UK sales – £27,200.00
   - Exports (outside EU) – £9,705.00
   - Despatches (within EU) to VAT-registered customers – £18,345.00
   - Despatches (within EU) to non-VAT-registered customers – £7,200.00

Complete the following extract of the VAT return.

VAT return for quarter ended 31.03.20X0		£
VAT due in this period on **sales** and other outputs	Box 1	
Total value of **sales** and all other outputs, excluding any VAT. **Include your box 8 figure. Whole pounds only**	Box 6	
Total value of all **supplies** of goods and related costs, excluding any VAT, to other **EC Member States. Whole pounds only**	Box 8	

8 Valerie is VAT-registered and purchases standard-rated items for her business, both in the UK and overseas. Purchases (excluding VAT) for the quarter ended 31.3.20X0 are split as follows:

   - UK purchases – £9,230.00
   - Imports (outside EU) – £1,205.00
   - Acquisitions (within EU) from VAT-registered suppliers – £8,345.00

Complete the following extract of the VAT return.

VAT return for quarter ended 31.03.20X0		£
VAT due in this period on **acquisitions** from other **EC Member States**	Box 2	
VAT reclaimed in the period on **purchases** and other inputs, including acquisitions from the EC	Box 4	
Total value of purchases and all other inputs excluding any VAT. **Include your box 9 figure. Whole pounds only**	Box 7	
Total value of all **acquisitions** of goods and related costs, excluding any VAT, from other **EC Member States. Whole pounds only**	Box 9	

VAT schemes for small businesses

Learning outcomes

1.3	Explain, for these VAT schemes: annual accounting; cash accounting; flat rate scheme; standard scheme:
	• The special VAT schemes that can be used by some registered businesses: the annual, standard and cash accounting schemes and the flat rate scheme for small businesses
	• The thresholds and qualification criteria for the special VAT schemes
	• Why being in the normal VAT scheme or in one or more of the special VAT schemes affect the timing and frequency of filing returns and payment of VAT

Assessment context

Task 3 will ask you questions in respect of the schemes. Details of VAT schemes will be provided in the reference material onscreen in the exam.

Qualification context

As an accounting technician, you will need to have an appreciation of schemes available for small businesses. You will not need to know the schemes in great detail but will need to be able to talk about them at a basic level.

Business context

Knowing what options are available to a business in respect of registering for VAT is important as there are schemes which can help cut the cost of administration.

Chapter overview

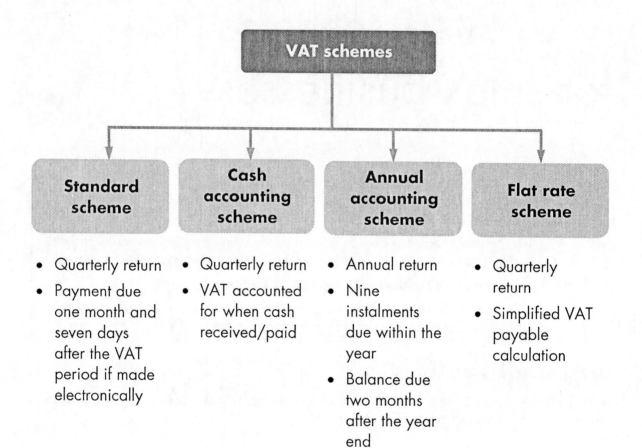

VAT schemes

Standard scheme
- Quarterly return
- Payment due one month and seven days after the VAT period if made electronically

Cash accounting scheme
- Quarterly return
- VAT accounted for when cash received/paid

Annual accounting scheme
- Annual return
- Nine instalments due within the year
- Balance due two months after the year end

Flat rate scheme
- Quarterly return
- Simplified VAT payable calculation

Introduction

When registering for VAT, there are several schemes that a business may be eligible to opt for. In the exam, you will be required to be able to explain whether a business is eligible for each scheme. The four schemes on your syllabus are:

(1)   The standard scheme
(2)   The cash accounting scheme
(3)   The annual accounting scheme
(4)   The flat rate scheme

1 The standard scheme

This is the scheme that a business is automatically entered into when it registers for VAT.

- VAT returns are completed on a quarterly basis.

- Repayment traders (eg, zero-rated suppliers) may opt to complete a VAT return each month.

- Payments are made one month and seven days from the end of the VAT period if the submission is electronic. This is reduced to one month from the end of the VAT period if it is a paper submission.

2 The cash accounting scheme

The **cash accounting scheme** enables businesses to ignore the tax point rules and account for VAT only when it is paid and received.

2.1 Conditions

- The scheme can only be used when a business's VAT-exclusive taxable turnover is not expected to exceed £1,350,000 in the next 12 months.

- Businesses will only be eligible if they are not a member of the flat rate scheme (see later).

- A taxable person can join the scheme only if all returns and VAT payments are up to date (or arrangements have been made to pay outstanding VAT by instalments).

- The taxable person must also not have been convicted of a VAT offence or penalty in the previous 12 months.

- Once in the scheme, if VAT-exclusive taxable supplies exceed £1,600,000 in the previous 12 months or next 12 months (estimated), notice must be given to HMRC within 30 days and the business must exit the cash accounting scheme (they may be able to use the scheme for a further 6 months).

2.2 Return and payment submission dates

The due dates are the same as for the standard scheme, unless the business has also entered into the annual accounting scheme.

2.3 Advantages

Output VAT is not paid to HMRC until it has been collected from the customer, leading to a cash flow advantage over the standard scheme. This is especially beneficial if the business offers long credit terms to customers, but pays its suppliers promptly.

Cash accounting gives automatic bad debt relief as the output VAT is only paid over to HMRC when it is received from the customer.

Activity 1: Julie Ltd – Cash accounting scheme

Julie Ltd receives cash for most of its sales, buys most of its purchases on credit and has an estimated turnover for the next 12 months of £1,200,000.

Required

(a) What is the turnover limit for ceasing to use the cash accounting scheme? Choose ONE answer.

    A   Estimated turnover in the next 12 months is more than £1,350,000.
    B   Estimated turnover in the next 12 months is more than £1,600,000.

(b) Is the business eligible to join the cash accounting scheme? Choose ONE answer.

    A   Yes
    B   No

3 The annual accounting scheme

The **annual accounting scheme** allows businesses to submit only one VAT return each year. They are still, however, required to make payments throughout the year.

3.1 Return and payment submission dates

The trader pays 90% of the prior year VAT liability (or of an estimate if this is the business's first year of trading) in nine equal instalments over months 4 to 12 of the year. Payment is due at the end of the relevant month and must be made by direct debit.

The remaining balance is settled two months after the year end and submitted with the VAT return form.

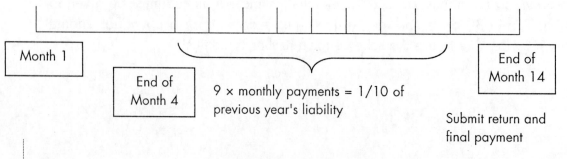

Month 1

End of Month 4

9 × monthly payments = 1/10 of previous year's liability

End of Month 14

Submit return and final payment

3.2 Conditions

- VAT-exclusive taxable turnover is not expected to exceed £1,350,000 in the next 12 months.

- All returns and VAT payments are up to date (or arrangements have been made to pay outstanding VAT by instalments).

- Once registered with the scheme, if VAT-exclusive taxable supplies exceed £1,600,000 in the previous 12 months, notice must be given to HMRC within 30 days and the business must leave the scheme.

3.3 Advantages of the annual accounting scheme

- Submitting only one VAT return reduces the administrative burden of VAT.

- The business has an extra month between the end of the VAT period and the return submission date.

- Paying a fixed amount on each instalment makes cash flow management easier.

3.4 Disadvantages of the annual accounting scheme

- If turnover decreases, the interim payments may be higher than they need to be.

- The business will have to wait until the end of the year when it submits its return for a refund.

Activity 2: Thelma Ray – Annual accounting scheme

Using the picklists over the page, complete the following email to a client who has had a small business for many years.

To: Thelma Ray
From: AN Accountant
Date: 15 October
Subject: Annual Accounting Scheme

Dear Thelma Ray,

Please be advised that based on your VAT liability for last year of £90,000, and the fact that your VAT year ends on 30 September, your payments for the next VAT year will be as follows:

Payments on Account

(1) [▾] will be payable at the end of each month for (2) [▾] months. The first payment will be due in (3) [▾].

Balancing Payment

The balancing payment and annual return will be due at the end of (4) [▾].

(5) [▾] will be payable if you expect your liability to increase by £12,000 next year.

Kind regards
AN Accountant

Picklists:

(1)	£9,000	£10,000	£7,500
(2)	12	6	9
(3)	January	March	October
(4)	March	November	September
(5)	£9,000	£12,000	£21,000

4 Flat rate scheme

The **flat rate scheme** makes the calculation of the VAT liability simpler, by calculating the amount of VAT payable as a flat (generally industry-specific) percentage of total VAT-inclusive turnover. If a trader has limited costs, the flat rate will be 16.5% of VAT-inclusive turnover. A limited cost trader is one whose purchases of goods are less than either:

- 2% of turnover, or
- £1,000 per year.

4.1 Conditions

- A business's **VAT-exclusive** taxable turnover is not expected to exceed £150,000 in the next 12 months.

- The business is not a member of the cash accounting scheme.

- If **VAT-inclusive** total supplies (including exempt supplies) exceed £230,000 in the previous 12 months, notice must be given to HMRC within 30 days and the business must leave the scheme.

4.2 Return and payment submission dates

The due dates are the same as for the standard scheme, unless the business has also entered into the annual accounting scheme.

The VAT payable is calculated in a completely different way than usual, by applying a flat rate percentage to the total VAT-inclusive turnover of all supplies, so no input VAT is reclaimable.

Output VAT is charged as normal to customers.

4.3 Advantages of the flat rate scheme

- VAT payable is normally less than the amount payable under the standard accounting scheme.

- There will be simplified administration as VAT does not have to be accounted for on each individual sales or purchase invoice.

- Cash flow can be managed as the VAT payable is a percentage of turnover.

Activity 3: Phyllis – Flat rate scheme

Phyllis, making only standard-rated supplies, wants to join the flat rate scheme.

The flat rate percentage applied to her business sector is 8%.

The VAT-exclusive turnover for the quarter is £40,000.

Phyllis also made purchases of £20,000, inclusive of standard rate VAT.

Required

(a) If Phyllis opted for the flat rate scheme, what would be the VAT payable for the quarter?

(b) If Phyllis didn't opt for the flat rate scheme, what would be the VAT payable for the quarter? (To the nearest £1.)

Solution

Chapter summary

- If a VAT-registered business has an annual VAT-exclusive turnover of no more than £1,350,000, it may be eligible for the cash accounting scheme – under which VAT has to be accounted for to HMRC on the basis of cash payments received and made, rather than under the normal tax point rules.

- If a VAT-registered business has an annual VAT-exclusive turnover of no more than £1,350,000, it may be eligible for the annual accounting scheme – under which nine monthly direct debit payments are made, usually based on the previous year's VAT liability. The balancing payment is made when the VAT return for the year is submitted within two months of the year end.

- If a VAT-registered business has an annual VAT-exclusive turnover of no more than £150,000, it may be eligible for the flat rate scheme – under which it can simplify its VAT records by calculating its VAT payment as a percentage of total (VAT-inclusive) turnover instead of recording the input and output tax on each individual purchase and sales invoice.

Keywords

- **Annual accounting scheme:** A method of accounting for VAT which does not require quarterly returns and payments, but instead requires nine monthly direct debit payments and one annual return, accompanied by the final balancing payment

- **Cash accounting scheme:** A method of accounting for VAT which allows VAT to be dealt with according to the date of payment or receipt of cash, rather than under the normal tax point rules

- **Flat rate scheme:** Enables businesses to calculate their VAT payment as a percentage of total VAT-inclusive turnover

1   **Using the picklist below, complete the following letter concerning the annual accounting scheme to Jacob Lymstock, a client of yours who has had a small business for several years.**

AN Accountant
Number Street
London
SW11 8AB

Mr Lymstock
Alphabet Street
London
W12 6WM

Dear Mr Lymstock

ANNUAL ACCOUNTING SCHEME

I have recently been reviewing your files. I would like to make you aware of a scheme that you could use for VAT.

As the annual value of your taxable supplies, (1) [____▼] VAT, in the following 12 months is expected to be (2) [____▼] (3) [____▼] you can join the annual accounting scheme.

Under this scheme, you make (4) [____▼] monthly direct debit payments based on your VAT liability for the previous year. The first of these payments is due at the end of the (5) [____▼] month of the accounting period. You must then prepare a VAT return for the year and submit it with the balancing payment by (6) [____▼] after the year end.

Use of this annual accounting scheme is a great help, as it means that you only have to prepare (7) [____▼] VAT return(s) each year.

If you wish to discuss this with me in more detail, please do not hesitate to contact me.

Yours sincerely

AN Accountant

Picklists:

(1)	including	excluding	
(2)	no more than	greater than	
(3)	£1,350,000	£1,600,000	
(4)	4	9	10	12
(5)	first	fourth	twelfth
(6)	30 days	one month	two months
(7)	1	4	12

2   **Complete the following statements about the cash accounting scheme using the picklists below.**

If the annual value of taxable supplies, (1) [____▼] VAT, is (2) [____▼] than (3) [____▼], provided that a trader has a clean record with HMRC, he may be able to apply to use the cash accounting scheme.

The scheme allows the accounting for VAT to be based on the date of (4) [____▼]. This is particularly useful for a business which gives its customers a (5) [____▼] period of credit while paying its suppliers promptly.

The scheme also gives automatic relief (6) [____▼], so if the customer does not pay the amount due, then the VAT need not be accounted for to HMRC.

Picklists:

(1)	including	excluding
(2)	no more	greater
(3)	£1,350,000	£1,600,000
(4)	receipt and payment of money	invoice
(5)	long	short
(6)	from filing VAT returns	for bad debts

3   An existing trader makes standard-rated supplies and uses the flat rate scheme. The flat rate percentage that he must use is 11.5%.
For the quarter ended 31 March 20X0, the trader had total turnover of £9,500 excluding VAT. He also had VAT-exclusive purchases of £3,000.

(a)   **Which figure reflects the amount of VAT payable to HMRC? Tick the box with the correct answer.**

	✓
£897.00	
£1,092.50	
£1,311.00	

(b)   **In this quarter, would the trader have more or less VAT to pay to HMRC if he was not in the flat rate scheme? Tick the box with the correct answer.**

	✓
More VAT is payable not using the flat rate scheme.	
More VAT is payable using the flat rate scheme.	

4   A trader has joined the annual accounting scheme for the year ended 31 December 20X7.

Identify whether the following statement is true or false.

	True ✓	False ✓
The first payment due to HMRC is by 1 April 20X7.		

5   **Would the cash accounting scheme improve the cash flow of a retail business that receives most of its sales in cash and buys most of its purchases on credit? Tick ONE of the boxes.**

	✓
Yes, because they would be able to reclaim input VAT earlier.	
Yes, because they would pay output VAT later.	
No, because they would reclaim input VAT later.	
No, because they would pay output VAT earlier.	

6   A trader making standard-rated (20%) supplies has joined the flat rate scheme. The flat rate percentage applying to his business sector is 8.5%.

His VAT-exclusive turnover for the quarter is £30,000.

What is the VAT due to HMRC for the quarter?

	✓
£2,550	
£3,060	

Administration

7

Learning outcomes

Having studied this chapter you will be able to:

1.1	Identify and analyse relevant information on VAT
	• Relevant sources of VAT information needed by a business
	• How to analyse available information and identify relevant items to extract
	• How to communicate relevant regulatory information to others within the business
	• The ethical and legal implications of failure to identify and apply information and regulations to the business
1.2	Explain the necessary interaction with the relevant tax authority regarding:
	• Their powers to require businesses to comply with regulations about registration, record keeping, submissions of VAT returns and payment of VAT due
	• How and when it is appropriate to obtain guidance from the relevant tax authority about VAT matters, particularly in respect of issues where there is doubt over the correct treatment
	• Their rights in respect of inspection of records and control visits
1.5	Maintain knowledge of legislation, regulation, guidance and codes of practice
2.4	Make adjustments and declarations for any errors or omissions identified in previous VAT periods
3.1	Explain the implications for a business of failure to comply with registration requirements
3.2	Explain the implications for a business of failure to comply with the requirement to submit VAT returns
3.3	Explain the implications for a business of failure to comply with the requirement to make payment of VAT
4.1	Inform the appropriate person about VAT-related matters
4.2	Communicate information about VAT due to or from the tax authority

Assessment context

Task 4 may ask for information in respect of errors and penalties which relate to the VAT system. There is a lot of information within the reference material which is available in the assessment.

Task 8 will require you to complete a communication to either a client or HMRC using picklists.

Qualification context

As an accounting technician, you will need to be aware of the consequences of not completing VAT returns accurately or on time. You will also need to know how to communicate with clients or HMRC formally.

Business context

If tasks are not completed within a finance role, then there is a risk of the business being subject to penalties. It is important to know these consequences.

Formal communication will also be required for both internal and external communication, and it is a skill which requires practice.

Chapter overview

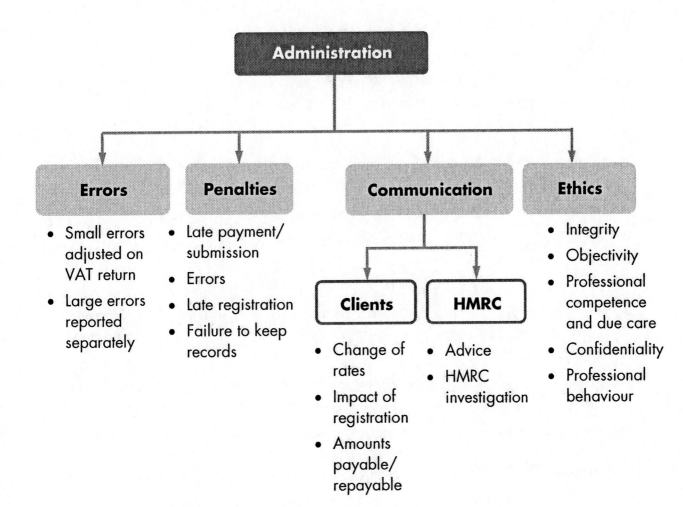

1 Errors

If a business discovers any errors on VAT returns which have already been submitted, then how we treat these errors will depend on their size and the cause of the error.

1.1 Deliberate errors

These need to be reported to HMRC separately. This is done by contacting the HMRC VAT Error Correction Team in writing and preferably using form VAT652.

1.2 Non-deliberate errors

These errors need to be added together to obtain the 'net' value of errors. This is calculated as any under-declaration of VAT, less any over-declaration of VAT.

The net error is then compared to the **error correction threshold**, which is the greater of:

- £10,000
- 1% of turnover (box 6 on the return) subject to an overall limit of £50,000.

If the net error is more than the **error correction 'threshold'**, then the HMRC VAT Error Correction Team will need to be contacted in the same way as for disclosing deliberate errors.

If the net error falls below this threshold, then the error can be adjusted on the next VAT return. A single adjustment is made for the net of all the errors.

The error correction threshold is in the AAT reference material provided in the exam.

Illustration 1: Correction of errors

A business recorded a credit note issued to a customer as showing VAT of £60.00 instead of the correct amount of £6.00. In the same VAT period, the business included a sales invoice with VAT of £300 twice in the sales day book.

The net error is:

	£
Output tax understated by £60.00 – £6.00	54.00
Output tax overstated by £300.00	(300.00)
Net error (overstatement of output tax)	246.00

Output tax in box 1 in the next VAT return should be reduced by £246.00 to correct this error.

Activity 1: Jim – VAT error

You discover that a sales invoice has been entered in Jim's records twice and so the VAT has been paid twice in the quarter ended 31 March 20X1. The amount of VAT is £450 and you are about to prepare the VAT return for the quarter ended 30 June 20X1. The box 6 figure on the last VAT return was £4,000.

Required

What action should you take? Choose ONE answer.

		✓
A	Ignore the error as it is less than 1% of the box 6 figure for the quarter ended 31 March 20X1.	
B	Add £450 to the box 1 figure for the VAT return for the quarter ended 30 June 20X1.	
C	Deduct £450 from the box 1 figure for the VAT return for the quarter ended 30 June 20X1.	
D	Obtain and complete form VAT652 'Notification of Errors in VAT Returns'.	

Workings

Activity 2: X Ltd error

X Ltd has turnover of £6.5 million. The output tax on its last VAT return was understated by £52,000.

Required

Tick ONE statement below.

	✓
A correction can be made on the next VAT return as the error is less than 1% of turnover.	
A correction cannot be made on the next return as the error exceeds £10,000.	
A correction cannot be made on the next return as the error exceeds £50,000.	

2 Penalties

HMRC ensures that taxable traders follow the VAT legislation by imposing fines and penalties when the trader is at fault. You need to have an awareness only of these penalties.

Wrongdoing	Disclosure
Careless and deliberate errors	The penalty charged for wrongdoing will be a percentage of the potential lost revenue (ie the VAT underpaid to HMRC). This will be charged on an error, whether it was reported separately or adjusted in the next VAT return. A trader can minimise these penalties by making unprompted disclosures to HMRC about the errors.
Inaccurate VAT returns	These penalties can be reduced to zero if the trader makes an unprompted disclosure to HMRC about the inaccuracies. If the return cannot be completed on time because some information is missing, HMRC will usually permit some of the figures to be estimated and corrected in the next return.
Late VAT return or payment	When this first occurs, the trader is said to be in default. A 12-month **surcharge liability notice** period is then started. If a late payment occurs within this period, a surcharge penalty is issued and the surcharge period is reset to 12 months. This will be a percentage of the VAT unpaid to HMRC.
Failure to register for VAT	Traders need to ensure that they are completing the historic and future tests on a regular basis. Once they have identified the need to register, they must do so within 30 days of the test date. The penalty will be based on a percentage of the VAT due from the date registration was supposed to occur.
Failure to keep and retain records	All records must be kept for at least six years, unless HMRC gives written permission for a shorter period. Where records have not been retained for this period, there is a maximum penalty of £3,000 per accounting period.

2.1 Assessments

The majority of penalties are based on the VAT which is due to HMRC.

If no VAT return is submitted, HMRC can raise an assessment based on what it believes is owed.

The penalty is then calculated on this amount.

The trader then has 30 days to notify HMRC if the amount owed is actually bigger. If this is not done, then they may be liable to another penalty.

2.2 Fraudulent evasion of VAT

Tax evasion is a criminal offence and this will result in fines and/or (in extreme cases) imprisonment.

Tax evasion of VAT:

- Misleading HMRC by suppressing information or deliberately providing false information
- Illegal

Tax avoidance:

- Using the legislation to minimise your tax burden
- Legal

3 Communications

In the exam, you will need to complete a written communication to HMRC or to a client.

This communication could be on anything you have seen in your VAT studies so far, ie contacting a client to discuss what VAT is payable to HMRC and when, or it could be in respect of the following.

3.1 Contact with HMRC

3.1.1 Seeking advice on VAT legislation

HMRC will expect taxpayers to go through the following process:

(a)   Check the **HMRC website** – this can usually resolve most queries.
(b)   Telephone the VAT helpline – with VAT registration number and postcode.
(c)   Write to HMRC – preferably by email.

Any communication must always be carried out in a polite and professional manner. You should always keep a record of any communication with HMRC.

3.1.2 Control visits

HMRC officers may visit a VAT-registered business to determine whether their VAT records are correct and up to date. They are entitled to do the following activities:

(a)   Question the business owner, or the person responsible for keeping the VAT records

(b)　Examine business records

(c)　Check the VAT return is accurate

(d)　Watch business activity

The officer will need to contact the business owner in writing at least seven days before the visit.

3.2 Maintaining up-to-date VAT knowledge

Tax advisers need to keep up to date with the VAT legislation to ensure that they keep their clients compliant and avoid penalties and surcharges.

Legislation changes can be found:

(a)　On the HMRC and government websites
(b)　In direct communications with HMRC
(c)　In technical circulars within accountancy firms
(d)　In specialist journals

Changes in practice may be identified by:

(a)　Attending continual professional development (CPD) briefings
(b)　Reading relevant journals
(c)　Meeting other professionals

3.3 Changes in VAT legislation

Changes to the VAT legislation can have an impact on a number of things.

3.3.1 Accounting systems

If the tax rate changes, in general or just for a specific product, then IT systems will need to be updated for the new rates.

3.3.2 Customers

If the business's customers are all VAT-registered, then the change in VAT will not impact them as they will be able to recover the input VAT they have suffered. However, if they are not VAT-registered, then an increase to the VAT rate will increase the cost of that product for the customer.

The supplier will have to consider whether to raise their prices (thus passing the VAT increase on to their customers) or to keep prices the same, and therefore retain less of the sales revenue. For example, an increase in the VAT rate from 20% to 22% on a net sale of £100 could be dealt with as follows:

Option 1: raise prices

The selling price would go from £120 (£100 × 120%) to £122 (£100 × 122%)

Option 2: keep prices the same

The previous selling price of £120 would now represent 122% of the net price. Therefore the trader would owe £21.64 (£120 × 22/122) to HMRC and would retain the remaining £98.36. The customer would not bear any of the additional VAT cost but the trader's net profit would fall.

3.3.3 Non-VAT-registered businesses

If the VAT registration threshold changes, then this could mean that some businesses may need to register earlier or later than expected.

Activity 3: Ian Morris – Client communication

You are a trainee accounting technician working for a sole trader, Mr Shelton. Mr Shelton has just received a letter from a client, Ian Morris (a trader making only standard-rated supplies to non-registered clients), asking about the impact of a recent change in the standard rate of VAT on his clients. The rate changed from 20% to 25%. He is undecided about whether to change his prices.

Required

You are required to complete the following letter to Ian Morris discussing the options open to him.

To: Ian Morris
From: Mr Shelton
Date: 30 December
Subject: Change of VAT rate

Dear Ian Morris,

Further to your recent email, I have set out below the options open to you in relation to the standard rate of VAT.

Until recently, you have been charging VAT at a rate of (1) [____ ▼]. Therefore a VAT-exclusive sale with a value of £1,000 has cost your non-registered clients (2) [____ ▼].

The two options open to you are as follows:

- Keep the same VAT-exclusive value of £1,000.

  The benefit of this option is that you have the same amount of VAT-exclusive sales value per item sold. However, this will now make the VAT-inclusive cost to your customers higher at (3) [____ ▼]. This may make your prices less competitive (if your competitors do not do the same) and may result in a loss of some customers.

- Keep the same VAT-inclusive value of (4) [____ ▼].

  Under this alternative option, you will remain competitive to your customers. However, your VAT-exclusive sales value per item sold will be reduced to (5) [____ ▼].

There is no obvious correct option to choose; it will depend primarily on the strength of your competitors.

If you wish to discuss this with me in more detail, please do not hesitate to contact me.

Yours sincerely,

Mr Shelton

Picklists:

(1)	0%	20%	25%
(2)	1,000	1,200	1,500
(3)	1,000	1,200	1,250
(4)	1,000	1,200	1,250
(5)	1,000	960	800

4 Ethics

4.1 Fundamental principles

Working in tax requires adherence to the following five fundamental ethical principles:

- **Integrity.** Being straightforward and honest in all business relationships.

- **Objectivity.** Refusing to allow bias, conflicts of interest or undue influence to override professional judgements.

- **Professional competence and due care.** A professional accountant has an obligation to keep their knowledge and skills at a level that enables clients to receive a competent professional service, and to act diligently when providing those services.

- **Confidentiality.** Respecting the confidentiality of client information, and keeping it confidential unless there is a legal or professional obligation to disclose it.

- **Professional behaviour.** Compliance with relevant laws and regulations to avoid discrediting the profession.

Activity 4: Fundamental principles

You work in the tax department of a large company. You have prepared the VAT return for the quarter, and submitted it to your Finance Director for her review. On reviewing your draft return, she has asked you to amend it in order reclaim all the VAT on a party, at which several clients were in attendance. She mentioned at the end of the conversation that your annual performance appraisal was due.

Required

Which fundamental principles could be breached if you agreed to her request?

Tick THREE boxes.

	✓
Integrity	
Objectivity	
Professional competence and due care	
Confidentiality	
Professional behaviour	

- If a net error smaller than the error correction reporting threshold is discovered from a previous tax period, it can be corrected in the next VAT return.

- If a net error exceeding the error correction reporting threshold is discovered from a previous tax period, it cannot be adjusted in the next VAT return. Instead, a voluntary disclosure should be made and the HMRC VAT Error Correction Team informed. A penalty might be imposed, depending on the behaviour of the business.

- If a VAT return or payment is late, the taxpayer is served with a surcharge liability notice which lasts for 12 months. If further payment defaults occur within that 12 months, there may be a surcharge to pay, and the notice is extended to 12 months again.

- A number of other penalties pertain to VAT, including for failure to register and failure to keep records.

- VAT evasion is a criminal offence and may give rise to fines and/or imprisonment.

- VAT can be a substantial payment for a business. Therefore steps must be taken to ensure both the return and any payment can be made by the due dates.

- Changes in VAT legislation can have a significant impact on accounting systems.

- Staff and customers need to be informed of a change to the VAT rate.

- HMRC expect taxpayers to try and resolve any queries by checking their website before telephoning or writing to them. However, sometimes written confirmation about an issue should be insisted upon.

- HMRC officers may, from time to time, visit a VAT-registered business to check on VAT records.

- It is important to maintain up-to-date knowledge of changes to VAT legislation and practice.

Keywords

- **Error correction threshold:** This is the threshold that dictates whether errors discovered on a previous return can be corrected on the next return or must be reported separately

- **Evasion of VAT:** Falsely reclaiming input VAT/understating output tax, obtaining bad debt relief or obtaining a repayment

- **HMRC website:** The first place a taxpayer must check to try and resolve any VAT queries

- **Surcharge liability notice:** This warns a business that its VAT return or payment was not received on time and if the business pays late within the next 12 months a default surcharge will be due

1 **Identify which one of the following statements is correct.**

	✓
If a net error of more than the lower of £10,000 and 1% of turnover (subject to an overall £5,000 limit) is discovered, it must be disclosed on form VAT652.	
If a net error of more than the greater of £10,000 and 1% of turnover (subject to an overall £5,000 limit) is discovered, it must be disclosed on form VAT652.	
If a net error of more than the lower of £10,000 and 1% of turnover (subject to an overall £50,000 limit) is discovered, it must be disclosed on form VAT652.	
If a net error of more than the greater of £10,000 and 1% of turnover (subject to an overall £50,000 limit) is discovered it must be disclosed on form VAT652.	

2 **Identify whether the following statement is true or false.**

	True ✓	False ✓
Tax avoidance is illegal and could lead to fines and/or imprisonment.		

3 You are a trainee accounting technician working for a sole trader, Mr Smith. Mr Smith has just received a letter from a client, Michael James (a trader making only standard-rated supplies to non-VAT-registered clients), asking about the impact of a recent change in the standard rate of VAT on his clients. The rate changed from 20% to 18%. He is undecided about whether to change his prices.

You are required to complete the following letter to Michael James, discussing the options open to him.

Mr Smith
Number Street
London
SW11 8AB

Mr James
Alphabet Street
London
W12 6WM

Dear Mr James

CHANGE IN THE STANDARD RATE OF VAT

Further to your recent letter, I have set out below the options open to you in relation to the standard rate of VAT.

Until recently, you have been charging VAT at a rate of (1) [▼]. Therefore a VAT-exclusive sale with a value of £1,000 has cost your non-VAT-registered clients (2) [▼] (£1,000 plus VAT).

The two options open to you are as follows:

- Keep the same VAT-exclusive value of £1,000.

  Under this option, you would have the same amount of VAT-exclusive sales value per item sold. However, this will now make the VAT-inclusive cost to your customers lower at (3) [▼] . You have effectively passed on the VAT saving to your customers.

- Keep the same VAT-inclusive value of (4) [▼] .

  Under this alternative option, you are not passing the VAT saving to your customers, which they may query, especially if your competitors reduce their prices. However, the benefit of this option is that your VAT-exclusive sales value per item sold will be increased to (5) [▼] .

There is no obvious correct option to choose; it will depend primarily on the actions of your competitors.

If you wish to discuss this with me in more detail, please do not hesitate to contact me.

Yours sincerely

Mr Smith

Picklists:

(1)	10%	20%	25%
(2)	1,000	1,200	1,250
(3)	£1,000	£1,200 (£1,000 plus VAT at 20%)	£1,180 (£1,000 plus VAT at 18%)
(4)	1,000	1,200	1,180
(5)	£1,000 (£1,200 × 100/120)	£1,016.95 (£1,200 × 100/118)	

4   **A taxpayer should try and resolve a VAT query in the following order.**

Fill in the blank space from the picklist below.

Firstly...	▼
If no luck, then...	▼
Still cannot resolve, then...	▼

Picklist:

check HMRC website.
ring the HMRC VAT helpline.
write to or email HMRC.

5   **Identify which one of the following statements is correct.**

	✓
A VAT officer will usually turn up for a control visit unannounced.	
A VAT officer can check the correct amount of VAT has been paid or reclaimed.	
A VAT officer is not entitled to examine the business records.	

6   A business made a 'small' overstatement of input tax on a previous return.

What effect will this have on the current VAT payable to HMRC?

	✓
An increase in the VAT payable via the current return.	
A decrease in the VAT payable via the current return.	
No impact on the current return. It must simply be separately declared.	

7   A business made a 'small' understatement of output tax on a previous return.

Should this adjustment be shown on the latest VAT return, and if so, where on the return?

	✓
No – not shown on the return	
Yes – shown in box 1	
Yes – shown in box 4	

8   **VAT account**

Date 20XX	Reference	Debit £	Date 20XX	Reference	Credit £
1.1–31.3	Sales returns day book	474.80	1.1–31.3	Sales day book	10,422.20
1.1–31.3	Purchases day book	3,596.00	1.1–31.3	Cash book – UK sales	2,069.00
31.3	Bad debt relief	195.00	1.1–31.3	Purchases returns day book – UK purchases	204.00
31.3	EU acquisition reclaim	651.20	31.3	Fuel scale charge	28.83
31.3	Balance b/d	8,458.23	31.3	EU acquisition charge	651.20
	Total	**13,375.23**		**Total**	**13,375.23**
				VAT payable	8,458.23

Following on from the example in Chapter 5, use the above VAT account to complete the email below.

To: Finance Director
From: Accounting Technician
Date: 25 April 20XX
Subject: VAT return to 31 March 20XX

Please be advised that I have now completed the VAT return for the quarter to 31 March 20XX. If you are in agreement with the figures shown in the return, please could you arrange an electronic payment of £ [   ] to be made by [▾].

If you wish to discuss this further, please feel free to call me.

Kind regards

Picklist:

30 April 20XX
7 May 20XX
7 June 20XX

9   Doug is a retailer and has been selling goods to the general public for £235 (VAT inclusive) while the VAT rate was 17.5% (VAT fraction 7/47). When the VAT rate changed to 20% he did not want to change the cost of these goods to his customers who are not VAT-registered.

Work out for Doug the VAT-exclusive amount of the goods sold both before and after the change in the VAT rate.

VAT inclusive £	VAT rate	VAT exclusive £
235.00	17.5%	
235.00	20%	

Activity answers

CHAPTER 1 Introduction to VAT

Activity 1: Input and output tax

	Input tax ✓	Output tax ✓
Business A		✓
Business B	✓	

CHAPTER 2 VAT basics

Activity 1: Cost to business

Business type	Type of supply made	Net cost £
Insurance company	Only exempt supplies	1,200
Accountancy firm	Only standard-rated supplies	1,000
Bus company	Only zero-rated supplies	1,000

Although the accountancy firm and bus company pay £1,200 for their telephone bills, they are able to reclaim the input VAT of £200, so the net cost is £1,000. The insurance company making exempt supplies is not able to reclaim input tax and so the net cost is £1,200.

Activity 2: Mark – Registration

(a) As his turnover in the last 12 months does not exceed £85,000 until 31 October 2020 (on a month-by-month basis) he does not become liable until then.

Working

12 months to 30 September = £82,800

12 months to 31 October = £82,800 + (£25,500/3) – (£18,000/3) = £85,300

(b) He must then notify the HMRC within 30 days, ie by 30 November 2020.

(c) He is then registered from 1 December 2020 or an earlier date by mutual agreement.

Activity 3: Registration scenarios

		Register now ✓	Monitor and register later ✓
A	A new business with an expected turnover of £8,000 per month for the next 12 months.		✓
B	An existing business with a total turnover of £79,000 for the last 11 months. Sales for the next 30 days are not yet known.		✓
C	An existing business with a total turnover of £7,500 per month for the last 12 months.	✓	

Workings

A   Monitor and register later, as neither the historic nor the future test have been exceeded at this point

B   Monitor and register later, as taxable supplies have not yet exceeded £85,000 in the last 12 months

C   Register now, as taxable supplies in the previous 12 months exceed £85,000

Activity 4: Voluntary registration

		✓
A	Preparation of VAT returns would be required.	✓
B	Customers would benefit by being able to claim back input VAT.	
C	The business would benefit by being able to claim back input VAT.	

Option C is factually correct; but VAT can only be claimed back once registered. Option B is not correct because VAT-registered customers would neither gain nor lose because they could reclaim VAT charged to them, and non-registered customers would be disadvantaged because they would be charged VAT they could not reclaim.

CHAPTER 3 Inputs and outputs

Activity 1: Calculation of VAT – Inclusive price

VAT $= 642.00 \times 1/6$

     $= £107.00$

Activity 2: Calculation of VAT – Rounding

VAT = £54.89 × 20%

= £10.978

= £10.97 (rounded down to the nearest penny)

Activity 3: Calculation of VAT – VAT payable

C   A is the amount deductible, B is the amount payable.

Working

	£
Output tax £1,800 × 1/6	300
Input tax £1,000 × 20%	(200)
VAT payable	100

Activity 4: Reclaiming input tax

Circumstance	Yes, can reclaim ✓	No, cannot reclaim ✓
Input tax incurred on entertaining prospective new UK client		✓
Input tax incurred on a new car for the top salesperson		✓
Input tax incurred on a car for use in a driving instruction business	✓	

Activity 5: Reclaiming input tax on private fuel

	True ✓	False ✓
A VAT-registered business can reclaim all the input VAT on road fuel if it keeps detailed records of business and private mileage, and makes no other adjustment.		✓
A VAT-registered business can reclaim all the input VAT on road fuel if it pays the appropriate fuel scale charge for private mileage.	✓	

Activity 6: Partially exempt trader – Calculation

Attributable to taxable supplies

	£
Directly allocated	20,000
Indirectly allocated:	
$3,000 \times \dfrac{114,573}{135,429}$ (85%)	2,550
Recoverable	22,550

Attributable to exempt supplies

	£
Directly allocated	700
Indirectly allocated:	
(3,000 – 2,550)	450
Recoverable (see Workings)	1,150

Workings

Monthly average   = 1,150 ÷ 3
                           = £383

This is < £625 per month.

Total input tax = £23,700. Relating to taxable supplies = £22,550 (above).

This is > 50%

Therefore all of the £1,150 exempt input tax is recoverable as well as the £22,550 attributed to taxable supplies.

Activity 7: Partially exempt trader – Multiple choice

C   All of the input VAT can be reclaimed, providing certain (*de minimis*) conditions are met.

Activity 8: Despatches

To VAT-registered traders	To non-VAT-registered traders	✓
Zero-rated	Zero-rated	
Standard-rated	Zero-rated	
Zero-rated	Standard-rated	✓
Standard-rated	Standard-rated	

CHAPTER 4 Accounting for VAT

Activity 1: Valid VAT invoice

	✓
Customer VAT registration number	
Supplier VAT registration number	✓
Total VAT-exclusive amount for each type of item sold	✓
Total VAT amount charged	✓
Total VAT-inclusive amount for each type of item sold	

Activity 2: Effect on VAT

	✓
Input tax will increase	✓
Input tax will decrease	
Output tax will increase	
Output tax will decrease	

Activity 3: Reclaiming input VAT

	True ✓	False ✓
A 'simplified' invoice can be used to reclaim input VAT.	✓	
A 'proforma' invoice can be used to reclaim input VAT.		✓

Activity 4: Settlement discounts

	✓
Issue a further invoice for £50 plus VAT	
Issue a credit note for £50 plus VAT	✓
Take no action	
Issue a credit note for £50 including VAT	

Activity 5: Credit note

	✓
Input tax will increase.	
Input tax will decrease.	
Output tax will increase.	
Output tax will decrease.	✓

Activity 6: Alex – Tax point

B   25 May 20X2

Ignore the proforma invoice (as this is not a VAT invoice).

The earliest date is then the payment date, which is therefore the actual tax point.

(Only the despatch date (basic tax point) is ever overridden by the invoice date.)

Activity 7: Bang Ltd – Tax point

(a) A   16 June 20X1

The deposit payment is the earliest date (ignoring the order date). This is never overridden by the invoice date.

(b) C   30 June 20X1

The despatch date is the earliest date relating to the balancing payment. Double check if the invoice was issued within 14 days. In this case, it was not; therefore the despatch date remains as the tax point.

Activity 8: Bad debt relief

	✓
The amount payable will increase.	
The amount payable will decrease.	✓

CHAPTER 5 The VAT return

Activity 1: Credit note – Impact on VAT

D   Output VAT will decrease.

When the original supply was made, output VAT would have been recorded. A credit note is now having the effect of reversing that sale, so the output VAT needs to be reversed down again.

Activity 2: Irrecoverable VAT – Impact on accounts

Description	Net £	VAT £	Total £	Reclaim input VAT?
Office supplies	200.00	40.00	240.00	**Yes**
Purchase of company car	19,250.00	3,850.00	23,100.00	**No**
Computer	550.00	110.00	660.00	**Yes**
UK business entertainment	1,000.00	200.00	1,200.00	**No**

Activity 3: Books of prime entry – Impact on VAT account

	Debit ✓	Credit ✓	£
VAT figures			
From the sales day book		✓	8,750.00
From the sales returns day book	✓		437.50
From the purchases day book	✓		5,250.00
From the purchases returns day book		✓	393.75
From the cash receipts book		✓	1,514.45
From the cash payments book	✓		837.55

Activity 4: Correction of errors

	✓
£7,950	
£11,700	✓

By entering the VAT paid debit of £3,750, on the credit side, the balance on the account is showing as £11,700 instead of the correct £4,200.

Date 20X0	Reference	Debit £	Date 20X0	Reference	Credit £
			31/3/X0	VAT payable	3,750.00
	VAT paid should be here!	VAT paid should be here!	**31/3/X0**	**VAT paid**	**3,750.00**
			30/6/X0	VAT payable	4,200.00
	Balance	11,700.00			
	Total	**11,700.00**		**Total**	**11,700.00**

Activity 5: David Ltd – VAT return

(a) £14.23 (W) (**Note.** This figure to be added to box 4.)

(b)

Box 1	VAT due in this period on **sales** and other outputs	13,960.56
Box 2	VAT due in this period on **acquisitions** from other **EC Member States**	900.00
Box 3	Total VAT due (**the sum of boxes 1 and 2**)	14,860.56
Box 4	VAT reclaimed in the period on **purchases** and other inputs, including acquisitions from the EC	10,240.35 (W)
Box 5	Net VAT to be paid to HM Revenue & Customs or reclaimed by you (**difference between boxes 3 and 4**)	4,620.21
Box 6	Total value of **sales** and all other outputs excluding any VAT. **Include your box 8 figure. Whole pounds only**	77,002
Box 7	Total value of **purchases** and all other inputs excluding any VAT. **Include your box 9 figure. Whole pounds only**	51,130
Box 8	Total value of all **supplies** of goods and related costs, excluding any VAT, to other **EC Member States. Whole pounds only**	7,201
Box 9	Total value of all **acquisitions** of goods and related costs, excluding any VAT, from other **EC Member States. Whole pounds only**	4,500

Working

	£
VAT on purchases	9,326.12
VAT on acquisitions	900.00
VAT on bad debt = £85.41 × 1/6	14.23
	10,240.35

CHAPTER 6 VAT schemes for small businesses

Activity 1: Julie Ltd – Cash accounting scheme

(a) B Estimated turnover in the next 12 months is more than £1,600,000

(b) A Yes

Activity 2: Thelma Ray – Annual accounting scheme

To: Thelma Ray
From: AN Accountant
Date: 15 October
Subject: Annual Accounting Scheme

Dear Thelma Ray,

Please be advised that based on your VAT liability for last year of £90,000, and the fact that your VAT year ends on 30 September, your payments for the next VAT year will be as follows:

Payments on Account

£9,000 will be payable at the end of each month for 9 months. The first payment will be due in January .

Balancing Payment

The balancing payment and annual return will be due at the end of November .

£21,000 (W) will be payable if you expect your liability to increase by £12,000 next year.

Kind regards

AN Accountant

Working

VAT liability for the year: £81,000 + £12,000 = £102,000

Less (£90,000/10) × 9 =   (£81,000)

Balancing payment   £21,000

Activity 3: Phyllis – Flat rate scheme

(a)   VAT-inclusive turnover: £40,000 × 120% = £48,000

VAT payable: £48,000 × 8% = £3,840

(b)

Output VAT:	£40,000 × 20%	£8,000
Input VAT:	£20,000 × 20/120	(£3,333)
Total VAT payable		£4,667

CHAPTER 7 Administration

Activity 1: Jim – VAT error

C   Deduct £450 from the box 1 figure for the VAT return for the quarter ended 30 June 20X1.

A is wrong as an error should never be ignored; the 1% threshold applies to whether the error can be rectified on the return or should be notified separately, not to whether the error should be corrected at all. B would duplicate the error and D is not required as the error is less than £10,000, which itself is greater than 1% of the box 6 figure (ie £40).

Activity 2: X Ltd error

	✓
A correction can be made on the next VAT return as the error is less than 1% of turnover.	
A correction cannot be made on the next return as the error exceeds £10,000.	
A correction cannot be made on the next return as the error exceeds £50,000.	✓

The error is less than 1% of turnover, but that is subject to an overall limit of £50,000.

Activity 3: Ian Morris – Client communication

To: Ian Morris
From: Mr Shelton
Date: 30 December
Subject: Change of VAT rate

Dear Ian Morris,

Further to your recent email, I have set out below the options open to you in relation to the standard rate of VAT.

Until recently, you have been charging VAT at a rate of **20%** . Therefore, a VAT-exclusive sale with a value of £1,000 has cost your non-registered clients **£1,200** .

The two options open to you are as follows:

- Keep the same VAT-exclusive value of £1,000.

  The benefit of this option is that you have the same amount of VAT-exclusive sales value per item sold. However, this will now make the VAT-inclusive cost to your customers higher at **£1,250** . This may make your prices less competitive (if your competitors do not do the same) and may result in a loss of some customers.

- Keep the same VAT-inclusive value of **£1,200** .

  Under this alternative option, you will remain competitive to your customers. However, your VAT-exclusive sales value per item sold will be reduced to **£960** **(W)**.

There is no obvious correct option to choose; it will depend primarily on the strength of your competitors.

If you wish to discuss this with me in more detail, please do not hesitate to contact me.

Yours sincerely,

Mr Shelton

Working

£1,200 × 100/125 = £960

Activity 4: Fundamental principles

	✓
Integrity	✓
Objectivity	✓
Professional competence and due care	
Confidentiality	
Professional behaviour	✓

Integrity: It would not be honest to knowingly reclaim an excessive amount of input tax.

Objectivity: Agreeing to the Finance Director's request because of the impact on job prospects would be to allow bias to affect judgement.

Professional behaviour: Submitting a tax return that does not follow tax law is illegal.

Test your learning: answers

CHAPTER 1 Introduction to VAT

1

	✓
HM Customs & Excise	
Inland Revenue	
HM Revenue & Customs	✓
HM Treasury	

2

	✓
Output VAT is the VAT charged by a supplier on the sales that are made by his business. Output VAT is collected by the supplier and paid over to HMRC.	✓
Output VAT is the VAT suffered by the purchaser of the goods which will be reclaimed from HMRC if the purchaser is VAT-registered.	

The other statement describes input VAT.

3   VAT is collected by HMRC throughout the manufacturing/supply chain for goods. Each VAT-registered business that buys, processes and then sells the goods pays the difference between the VAT on their sale and the VAT on their purchase over to HMRC.

CHAPTER 2 VAT Basics

1

	True ✓	False ✓
If a business supplies zero-rated services, then the business is not able to reclaim the VAT on its purchases and expenses from HMRC.		✓
A business makes zero-rated supplies. The cost to the business of its purchases and expenses is the VAT-exclusive amount.	✓	

2

	Register without delay ✓	Register within 30 days ✓	Monitor and register later ✓
An existing business with total turnover for the previous 11 months of £80,000. Sales for the next month are unknown at present.			✓
A new business with an expected turnover for the next 30 days of £90,000.	✓		
An existing business with total turnover for the previous 12 months of £7,250 per month.		✓	

3

AN Accountant
Number Street
London
SW11 8AB

Mrs Quirke
Alphabet Street
London
W12 6WM

Dear Mrs Quirke

VAT REGISTRATION

Further to our recent telephone conversation, set out below are the circumstances when you must register your business for VAT.

If the taxable turnover of your business at the end of a month, looking back no more than ⟨ **12** ⟩ months, has exceeded the registration limit of ⟨ **£85,000** ⟩, then the business must apply to register for VAT within 30 days.

Alternatively, if at any time, the taxable turnover (before any VAT is added) is expected to exceed the registration limit within the next ⟨ **30 days** ⟩ alone, then the business must apply to be registered for VAT without delay. This would be the situation if, for example, you obtained a large additional contract for, say, £88,000.

If you wish to discuss this in any more detail, please do not hesitate to contact me.

Yours sincerely
AN Accountant

4 **By what date will Amy exceed the threshold for VAT?**

30 April 2019

By what date must Amy register for VAT?

30 May 2019

VAT registration is required when taxable supplies (standard plus zero-rated supplies) exceed £85,000. Taxable supplies are £9,520 (£7,850 + £1,670) per month.

Amy exceeds this threshold after nine months, ie by 30 April 2019, as taxable supplies are then £85,680 (9 × £9,520).

5

	✓
At the beginning of month 12, Richard expects his taxable supplies to exceed £85,000 in the next 30 days.	
At the end of month 12, Richard's taxable supplies in the previous 12 months will have exceeded £85,000.	✓

The historic test is met at the end of month 12.

For the future test to be met, the taxable supplies in the next 30 days alone must exceed the threshold, ie the taxable supplies in the previous 11 months are not included. Therefore, the future test is not met here.

6

	✓
Preparation of VAT returns would be optional.	
Customers would benefit by being able to claim back input VAT.	
Business would benefit by being able to claim back input VAT.	✓

Once registered, even voluntarily, VAT returns will have to be completed.

VAT-registered customers would neither gain nor lose because they could reclaim VAT charged to them, and non-VAT-registered customers would be disadvantaged because they would be charged VAT they could not reclaim.

CHAPTER 3 Inputs and outputs

1

(a)

The VAT is	£	76.80

VAT   =   £384.00 × 20%

   =   £76.80

(b)

	Output tax ✓	Input tax ✓
Business C	✓	
Business D		✓

2

	✓
Staff party	
Car for sales manager	✓
Photocopier	
Entertaining UK clients	✓

3

VAT inclusive £	VAT at 20% £
42.88	7.14
96.57	16.09
28.20	4.70
81.07	13.51

(a)   £42.88 × 1/6   =   £7.14
(b)   £96.57 × 1/6   =   £16.09
(c)   £28.20 × 1/6   =   £4.70
(d)   £81.07 × 1/6   =   £13.51

4

	✓
The goods will be treated as standard-rated in the UK if the US-based business is VAT-registered.	
The goods will be treated as standard-rated in the UK, provided documentary evidence of the export is obtained within three months.	
The goods will be treated as zero-rated in the UK if the US-based business is VAT-registered.	
The goods will be treated as zero-rated in the UK, provided documentary evidence of the export is obtained within three months.	✓

5

Net £	VAT rate %	VAT £	Gross £
43.50	20	8.70	52.20
18.00	20	3.60	21.60

Workings

1   VAT =   £52.20 × 1/6

        =   £8.70

2   VAT =   £18.00 × 20%

        =   £3.60

6

	True ✓	False ✓
A VAT-registered business can reclaim all the input VAT attributed to zero-rated supplies.	✓	
A VAT-registered business can reclaim all the input VAT attributed to standard-rated supplies.	✓	
A VAT-registered business can reclaim all the input VAT attributed to exempt supplies.		✓
A VAT-registered business can reclaim all the input VAT attributed to both taxable and exempt supplies providing certain *de minimis* tests are satisfied.	✓	

7

	✓
No VAT is charged by the EU supplier; therefore this can be ignored by Joe on his VAT return.	
Joe must pay output VAT to HMRC at the port/airport and can reclaim input VAT on the next return.	
Joe must charge himself 'output VAT' and reclaim 'input' VAT on the same return.	✓

CHAPTER 4 Accounting for VAT

1

	✓
1 year	
2 years	
6 years	✓
20 years	

2

	✓
A proforma invoice is always sent out when goods are sent to customers, before issuing the proper invoice.	
A proforma invoice should always include the words 'This is not a VAT invoice'.	✓
A customer can reclaim VAT stated on a proforma invoice.	
A proforma invoice is sent out to offer a customer the chance to purchase the goods detailed.	✓

3

	Date	Basic (B)/ Actual (A)
An invoice is sent out to a customer for goods on 22 June 20X0 and the goods are despatched on 29 June 20X0.	22 June	A
Goods are sent out to a customer on 18 June 20X0 and this is followed by an invoice on 23 June 20X0.	23 June	A
A customer pays in full for goods on 27 June 20X0 and they are then delivered to the customer on 2 July 20X0.	27 June	A

4

	✓
15 May 20X0	
20 May 20X0	✓
20 June 20X0	

The earliest date is the despatch on 15 May. As the invoice is sent within 14 days, the invoice date becomes the tax point.

5

	✓
2 June 20X0	✓
11 June 20X0	✓
29 June 20X0	
31 July 20X0	

Deposit

The cash paid for the deposit is the earliest date so 2 June is the tax point for the deposit.

Balance

Despatch is the earliest date relating to the balancing payment. This is not overridden by the invoice date as the invoice is sent more than 14 days later. So the despatch date of 11 June is the tax point for the balancing payment.

6

The VAT on a bad debt can be reclaimed from HMRC when the following conditions are met:

- The debt is more than six months overdue and less than four years and six months old.

- The original VAT on the invoice has been paid to HMRC.

- The debt is written-off in the accounts of the business.

CHAPTER 5 The VAT return

1

	True ✓	False ✓
If input VAT is greater than output VAT on the return, VAT is payable to HMRC.		✓
If output VAT is greater than input VAT on the return, VAT is repayable from HMRC.		✓

If input VAT is greater than output VAT on the return, then VAT is repayable, and if output VAT is greater than input VAT on the return, then VAT is payable to HMRC.

2

	✓
The payment of £4,700 for the previous quarter has been included twice in the VAT account.	
The payment of £4,700 for the previous quarter has been omitted from the VAT account.	✓

By omitting the VAT paid debit of £4,700, the balance on the account is showing as £12,220 instead of the correct £7,520.

Date 20XX	Reference	Debit £	Date 20XX	Reference	Credit £
QTR 1	VAT paid		QTR 1	VAT payable	4,700.00
			QTR 2	VAT payable	7,520.00
	Balance	12,220.00			
	Total	**12,220.00**		**Total**	**12,220.00**
			QTR 2	VAT payable	12,220.00

3

VAT return for quarter ended 30.06.20XX		£
VAT due in this period on **sales** and other outputs	Box 1	7,520.00
VAT due in this period on **acquisitions** from other **EC Member States**	Box 2	750.00
Total VAT due (**the sum of boxes 1 and 2**)	Box 3	8,270.00
VAT reclaimed in this period on **purchases** and other inputs, including acquisitions from the EC	Box 4	3,950.00
Net VAT to be paid to HM Revenue & Customs or reclaimed by you (**difference between boxes 3 and 4 – if box 4 is greater than box 3, use a minus sign**)	Box 5	4,320.00
Total value of **sales** and all other outputs, excluding any VAT. **Include your box 8 figure. Whole pounds only**	Box 6	43,400.00
Total value of **purchases** and all other inputs, excluding any VAT. **Include your box 9 figure. Whole pounds only**	Box 7	19,250.00
Total value of all **supplies** of goods and related costs, excluding any VAT, to other **EC Member States. Whole pounds only**	Box 8	0.00
Total value of all **acquisitions** of goods and related costs, excluding any VAT, from other **EC Member States. Whole pounds only**	Box 9	3,750.00

Workings

		£
Box 1	VAT on sales from the sales day book	5,200.00
	VAT on sales from the cash book	2,800.00
	Less VAT on credit notes	(480.00)
		7,520.00
Box 2	VAT due on EU acquisitions	750.00
Box 3	Total of box 1 and box 2 £7,520.00 + £750.00	8,270.00

		£
Box 4	VAT on purchases from purchases day book	3,100.00
	VAT on EU acquisitions	750.00
	Bad debt relief (£500.00 × 20%)	100.00
		3,950.00
Box 5	Net VAT due box 3 minus box 4	
	£8,270.00 – £3,950.00	4,320.00
Box 6	Standard-rated credit UK sales	26,000.00
	Less standard-rated credit notes	(2,400.00)
	Cash sales	14,000.00
	Exports	5,800.00
		43,400.00
Box 7	Standard-rated credit purchases	15,500.00
	EU acquisitions	3,750.00
		19,250.00
Box 8	EU sales	0.00
Box 9	EU acquisitions	3,750.00

4

VAT return for quarter ended 31.05.20XX		£
VAT due in this period on **sales** and other outputs	Box 1	7,066.78
VAT due in this period on **acquisitions** from other **EC Member States**	Box 2	0.00
Total VAT due **(the sum of boxes 1 and 2)**	Box 3	7,066.78
VAT reclaimed in this period on **purchases** and other inputs, including acquisitions from the EC	Box 4	4,735.17
Net VAT to be paid to HM Revenue & Customs or reclaimed by you **(difference between boxes 3 and 4 – if box 4 is greater than box 3, use a minus sign)**	Box 5	2,331.61
Total value of **sales** and all other outputs excluding any VAT. **Include your box 8 figure. Whole pounds only**	Box 6	38,890.00

VAT return for quarter ended 31.05.20XX		£
Total value of **purchases** and all other inputs excluding any VAT. **Include your box 9 figure. Whole pounds only**	Box 7	26,154.00
Total value of all **supplies** of goods and related costs, excluding any VAT, to other **EC Member States. Whole pounds only**	Box 8	0.00
Total value of all **acquisitions** of goods and related costs, excluding any VAT, from other **EC Member States. Whole pounds only**	Box 9	0.00

Tutorial note. In past assessments, the entries for boxes 6–9 have been accepted whether rounded up or down to the nearest pound. However, if the task does give particular instructions on rounding, then these instructions should be followed.

Workings

		£
Box 1	VAT on sales from the sales day book	6,135.65
	VAT on sales from the cash book	1,010.90
	Less VAT on credit notes	(79.77)
		7,066.78
Box 2	VAT due on EU acquisitions	0.00
Box 3	Total of box 1 and box 2	7,066.78
Box 4	VAT on purchases from purchases day book	4,090.17
	VAT on purchases from cash payments book	606.60
	Bad debt relief	38.40
		4,735.17
Box 5	Net VAT due box 3 minus box 4	2,331.61
Box 6	Zero-rated credit UK sales	3,581.67
	Standard-rated credit UK sales	30,678.25
	Cash sales	5,054.51
	Less zero-rated credit notes	(25.59)
	Less standard-rated credit notes	(398.86)
		38,890.00

	£
Box 7	Zero-rated credit UK purchases	2,669.80
	Standard-rated credit UK purchases	20,450.85
	Cash purchases	3,033.01
		26,154.00
Box 8	EU sales	0.00
Box 9	EU acquisitions	0.00

5

	✓
Input tax paid at the ports is reclaimed as input tax on the VAT return.	
Both input tax and output tax in relation to the goods are shown on the VAT return.	✓
They are zero-rated and so no VAT features on the VAT return.	
They are exempt and so no VAT features on the VAT return.	

6

	✓
The fuel scale charge increases output VAT and is shown in box 1.	✓
VAT on EU acquisitions increases both input VAT and output VAT and is shown in boxes 1 and 4.	
Credit notes received from suppliers reduce input VAT and are shown in box 4.	✓
Credit notes issued to customers reduce output VAT and are shown in box 1.	✓

VAT on EU acquisitions increases both input VAT and output VAT, but is shown in boxes 2 and 4.

7

VAT return for quarter ended 31.03.20X0		£
VAT due in this period on **sales** and other outputs	Box 1	6,880.00
Total value of **sales** and all other outputs, excluding any VAT. **Include your box 8 figure. Whole pounds only**	Box 6	62,450.00
Total value of all **supplies** of goods and related costs, excluding any VAT, to other **EC Member States. Whole pounds only**	Box 8	18,345.00

Box 1 = (27,200 + 7,200) × 20%

Box 6 = 27,200 + 9,705 + 18,345 + 7,200

Box 8 = 18,345

8

VAT return for quarter ended 31.03.20X0		£
VAT due in this period on **acquisitions** from other **EC Member States**	Box 2	1,669.00
VAT reclaimed in this period on **purchases** and other inputs, including acquisitions from the EC	Box 4	3,756.00
Total value of purchases and all other inputs excluding any VAT. **Include your box 9 figure. Whole pounds only**	Box 7	18,780.00
Total value of all **acquisitions** of goods and related costs, excluding any VAT, from other **EC Member States. Whole pounds only**	Box 9	8,345.00

Box 2 = 8,345 × 20%

Box 4 = (9,230 + 1,205 + 8,345) × 20%

Box 7 = 9,230 + 1,205 + 8,345

Box 9 = 8,345

1

AN Accountant
Number Street
London
SW11 8AB

Mr Lymstock
Alphabet Street
London
W12 6WM

Dear Mr Lymstock

ANNUAL ACCOUNTING SCHEME

I have recently been reviewing your files. I would like to make you aware of a scheme that you could use for VAT.

As the annual value of your taxable supplies, **excluding** VAT, in the following 12 months is expected to be **no more than** **£1,350,000** you can join the annual accounting scheme.

Under this scheme, you make **9** monthly direct debit payments based on your VAT liability for the previous year. The first of these payments is due at the end of the **fourth** month of the accounting period. You must then prepare a VAT return for the year and submit it with the balancing payment by **two months** after the year end.

Use of this annual accounting scheme is a great help, as it means that you only have to prepare **1** VAT return(s) each year.

If you wish to discuss this with me in more detail, please do not hesitate to contact me.

Yours sincerely

AN Accountant

2

If the annual value of taxable supplies, **excluding** VAT, is **no more** than **£1,350,000**, provided that a trader has a clean record with HMRC, he may be able to apply to use the cash accounting scheme.

The scheme allows the accounting for VAT to be based on the date of **receipt and payment of money**. This is particularly useful for a business which gives its customers a ┌ **long** ┐ period of credit while paying its suppliers promptly.

The scheme also gives automatic relief ┌ **for bad debts** ┐ so if the customer does not pay the amount due, then the VAT need not be accounted for to HMRC.

3

(a)

	✓
£897.00	
£1,092.50	
£1,311.00	✓

Working

£9,500 × 120% × 11.5% = £1,311.00

(b)

	✓
More VAT is payable not using the flat rate scheme.	
More VAT is payable using the flat rate scheme.	✓

Working

If not using the flat rate scheme, the VAT payable would be:

		£
Output tax	£9,500 × 20%	1,900.00
Input tax	£3,000 × 20%	(600.00)
		1,300.00

4

	True ✓	False ✓
The first payment due to HMRC is by 1 April 20X7.		✓

The first payment due to HMRC is by 30 April 20X7 (ie the **end** of month 4).

5

	✓
Yes, because they would be able to reclaim input VAT earlier.	
Yes, because they would pay output VAT later.	
No, because they would reclaim input VAT later.	✓
No, because they would pay output VAT earlier.	

6

	✓
£2,550	
£3,060	✓

The VAT due to HMRC is 8.5% of the VAT-inclusive figure.

(£30,000 × 120%) × 8.5% = £3,060

CHAPTER 7 Administration

1

The correct statement is:

	✓
If a net error of more than the lower of £10,000 and 1% of turnover (subject to an overall £5,000 limit) is discovered, it must be disclosed on form VAT652.	
If a net error of more than the greater of £10,000 and 1% of turnover (subject to an overall £5,000 limit) is discovered, it must be disclosed on form VAT652.	
If a net error of more than the lower of £10,000 and 1% of turnover (subject to an overall £50,000 limit) is discovered, it must be disclosed on form VAT652.	
If a net error of more than the greater of £10,000 and 1% of turnover (subject to an overall £50,000 limit) is discovered, it must be disclosed on form VAT652.	✓

2

	True ✓	False ✓
Tax avoidance is illegal and could lead to fines and/or imprisonment.		✓

Tax **evasion** is illegal and could lead to fines and/or imprisonment, as opposed to tax **avoidance**.

3

Mr Smith
Number Street
London
SW11 8AB

Mr James
Alphabet Street
London
W12 6WM

Dear Mr James

CHANGE IN THE STANDARD RATE OF VAT

Further to your recent letter, I have set out below the options open to you in relation to the standard rate of VAT.

Until recently, you have been charging VAT at a rate of $\boxed{\textbf{20\%}}$. Therefore a VAT-exclusive sale with a value of £1,000 has cost your non-VAT-registered clients $\boxed{\textbf{£1,200}}$ (£1,000 plus VAT).

The two options open to you are as follows:

- Keep the same VAT-exclusive value of $\boxed{\textbf{£1,000}}$.

  Under this option, you would have the same amount of VAT-exclusive sales value per item sold. However, this will now make the VAT-inclusive cost to your customers lower at $\boxed{\textbf{£1,180 (£1,000 plus VAT at 18\%)}}$. You have effectively passed on the VAT saving to your customers.

- Keep the same VAT-inclusive value of $\boxed{\textbf{£1,200}}$

  Under this alternative option, you are not passing the VAT saving to your customers, which they may query, especially if your competitors reduce their prices. However, the benefit of this option is that your VAT-exclusive sales value per item sold will be increased to $\boxed{\textbf{£1,016.95 (£1,200} \times \textbf{100/118)}}$.

There is no obvious correct option to choose; it will depend primarily on the actions of your competitors.

If you wish to discuss this with me in more detail, please do not hesitate to contact me.

Yours sincerely

Mr Smith

4

A taxpayer should try and resolve a VAT query in the following order:

Firstly...	check HMRC website.
If no luck, then...	ring the HMRC VAT helpline.
Still cannot resolve, then...	write to or email HMRC.

5

	✓
A VAT officer will usually turn up for a control visit unannounced.	
A VAT officer can check the correct amount of VAT has been paid or reclaimed.	✓
A VAT officer is not entitled to examine the business records.	

6

	✓
An increase in the VAT payable via the current return.	✓
A decrease in the VAT payable via the current return.	
No impact on the current return. It must simply be separately declared.	

7

	✓
No – not shown on the return	
Yes – shown in box 1	✓
Yes – shown in box 4	

It is shown as an increase in the output tax in box 1 on the VAT return.

8

To: Finance Director
From: Accounting Technician
Date: 25 April 20XX
Subject: VAT return to 31 March 20XX

Please be advised that I have now completed the VAT return for the quarter to 31 March 20XX. If you are in agreement with the figures shown in the return, please could you arrange an electronic payment of   £ | **8,458.23**

to be made by   **7 May 20XX** .

If you wish to discuss this further, please feel free to call me.

Kind regards

9

VAT inclusive £	VAT rate	VAT exclusive £
235.00	17.5%	200.00
235.00	20%	195.83

Workings

1   VAT rate of 17.5% (VAT fraction 7/47 or 17.5/117.5)

VAT-exclusive value £235 – (7/47 × £235) = £200

2   VAT rate of 20% (VAT fraction 1/6 or 20/120)

VAT-exclusive value £235 – (1/6 × £235) = £195.83

Tax reference material FA 2019

Introduction

This document comprises data that you may need to consult during your Indirect Tax computer-based assessment.

The material can be consulted during the sample and live assessments through pop-up windows. It is made available here so you can familiarise yourself with the content before the test.

Do not take a print of this document into the exam room with you*.

This document may be changed to reflect periodical updates in the computer-based assessment, so please check you have the most recent version while studying. This version is based on Finance Act 2019 and is for use in AAT assessments 1 January – 31 December 2020.

*Unless you need a printed version as part of reasonable adjustments for particular needs, in which case you must discuss this with your tutor at least six weeks before the assessment date.

Contents

	Page
Introduction to VAT	147
Rates of VAT	148
Registration and deregistration	150
Keeping business and VAT records	152
Exempt and partly-exempt businesses	154
Place of supply	155
Tax points	156
VAT invoices	158
Entertainment expenses	163
Vehicles and motoring expenses	164
Transactions outside the UK	165
Bad debts	166
Completing the online VAT Return, box by box	167
VAT periods, submitting returns and paying VAT	169
Special accounting schemes	172
Errors in previous VAT Returns	176
Surcharges, penalties and assessments	178
Finding out more information about VAT	179
Visits by VAT officers	179

Introduction to VAT

VAT is a tax that is charged on most goods and services that VAT-registered businesses provide in the UK. It is also charged on goods and some services that are imported from countries outside the European Union (EU), and brought into the UK from other EU countries.

Please note that underlying legislation on VAT is an EU directive. If Brexit were to occur then this may trigger significant changes to VAT in the UK.

VAT is charged when a VAT-registered business sells taxable goods and services to either another business or to a non-business customer. This is called output tax.

When a VAT-registered business buys taxable goods or services for business use it can generally reclaim the VAT it has paid. This is called input tax.

Her Majesty's Revenue and Customs (HMRC) is the government department responsible for operating the VAT system. Payments of VAT collected are made by VAT-registered businesses to HMRC.

Rate of VAT

There are three rates of VAT, depending on the goods or services the business provides. The rates are:

- standard rate – 20%. The standard-rate VAT fraction for calculating the VAT element of a gross supply is 20/120 or 1/6

- reduced – 5%.

- zero – 0%.

There are also some goods and services that are:

- exempt from VAT
- outside the scope of VAT (outside the UK VAT system altogether)

Taxable supplies

Zero-rated goods and services count as taxable supplies and are part of taxable turnover, but no VAT is added to the selling price because the VAT rate is 0%. If the business sells goods and services that are exempt, no VAT is added as they're not taxable supplies and they're also not taxable turnover.

Generally, a business cannot register for VAT or reclaim the VAT on purchases if it only sells exempt goods and services. Where some of its supplies are of exempt goods and services, the business is referred to as partially exempt. It may not be able to reclaim the VAT on all of its purchases.

A business which buys and sells only - or mainly - zero-rated goods or services can apply to HMRC to be exempt from registering for VAT. This could make sense if the business pays little or no VAT on purchases.

Taxable turnover

Taxable turnover consists of standard-rated sales plus all reduced-rated and zero-rated sales but excludes the VAT on those sales, exempt sales and out-of-scope sales. If one VAT-registered business acquires another business it immediately absorbs the turnover of that business, whether the acquired business is registered for VAT or not. All VAT decisions must thereafter be made based on the combined turnover.

Change in VAT rate

Generally a business must use the VAT rate applicable from the time of the legislative change, unless payment has already been received or the goods have already been delivered. In these cases a tax point has already been created and the rate applicable will have been set by the tax point.

An exception arises where the goods have been delivered, or otherwise removed by the customer, the supplier has elected to follow the 14-day rule for issuing VAT invoices and the VAT rate increases between the date of delivery of the goods and the issuing of the invoice. In this case it is the new VAT rate which applies.

Immediately after the rate change a business may opt to honour supplies of goods and services at the rate which applied when the contract to supply was agreed, however output tax is still accountable at the new rate.

If the business offers a prompt payment discount and opts to issue a credit note to cover the reduction in payment made by the customer then a change in VAT rate which occurs between the issue of the original invoice and final payment will not be affected by the change in VAT rate. The rate due on the credit note, issued to account for the reduced payment made, will be fixed by the tax point of the original invoice.

Registration and deregistration

Registration threshold

If at the end of any month taxable turnover for the previous 12 months is more than the current registration threshold of £85,000, the business must register for VAT within 30 days. Registration without delay is required if, at any time, the value of taxable turnover in the next 30 day period alone is expected to be more than the registration threshold.

A business which has trading that temporarily takes it above the VAT threshold of £85,000 but which expects turnover to drop back below the threshold almost immediately can apply to stay unregistered, but the business must be able to prove to HMRC that the momentary increase is a true one-off occurrence.

If trading is below the registration threshold

If taxable turnover has not crossed the registration threshold, the business can still apply to register for VAT voluntarily.

Deregistration threshold

The deregistration threshold is £83,000. If taxable turnover for the previous 12 months is less than or equal to £83,000, or if it is expected to fall to £83,000 or less in the next 12 months, the business can either:

- voluntarily remain registered for VAT, or
- ask HMRC for its VAT registration to be cancelled.

Failure to register

A business which fails to register when it is required to do so may face a civil penalty. More importantly HMRC will treat the business as though it had registered on time and will expect VAT to be accounted for as if it had been charged. The business has two choices in respect of this VAT, which it has not included in its invoices.

It may either:

- allow HMRC to treat the invoices as VAT inclusive and absorb the VAT which should have been charged, or

- account for VAT as an addition to the charges already invoiced and attempt to recover this VAT from its customers.

Cancellation of VAT registration

A registration must be cancelled if the business is closed down or ceases to make taxable supplies. If a business is being taken over by a business with a completely different structure, for example an unincorporated business being taken over by an incorporated business or vice versa, the original registration must be cancelled.

It will either be replaced by a new registration for the new business, or be subsumed into the registration of the expanded business. In some circumstances the new business may apply for the registration of the business being taken over to be re-allocated to the new business.

This may happen because two businesses merge and only one is currently registered. Re-allocation of the existing registration may be the most appropriate method of dealing with VAT registration.

Changes to the VAT registration

Some business changes will necessitate a change in details of the VAT registration, such as a change in the trading name or the address of the business. Other reasons for changes to the registration are a change in main business activities, particularly if this means a significant change to the types of supply, and changes to the business bank account details.

Failure to notify HMRC of changes which either cancel or change registration within 30 days of the relevant change may render the business and its owners liable to a civil penalty.

Keeping business and VAT records

All VAT-registered businesses must keep certain business and VAT records.

These records are not required to be kept in a set way, provided they:

- are complete and up to date

- allow the correct amount of VAT owed to HMRC or by HMRC to be worked out

- are easily accessible when an HMRC visit takes place, e.g. the figures used to fill in the VAT Return must be easy to find.

Business records

Business records which must be kept include the following:

- annual accounts, including statements of profit or loss
- bank statements and paying-in slips
- cash books and other account books
- orders and delivery notes
- purchases and sales day books
- records of daily takings such as till rolls
- relevant business correspondence.

VAT records

'In addition to the business records detailed in 7.1, VAT records must also be kept.

In general, the business must keep the following VAT records:

- records of all the standard-rated, reduced-rated, zero-rated and exempt goods and services that are bought and sold.

- copies of all sales invoices issued. However, businesses do not have to keep copies of any less detailed (simplified) VAT invoices for items under £250 including VAT

- all purchase invoices for items purchased for business purposes unless the gross value of the supply is £25 or less and the purchase was from a coin-operated telephone or vending machine, or for car parking charges or tolls.

- all credit notes and debit notes received.

- copies of all credit notes and debit notes issued.

- records of any goods or services bought for which there is no VAT reclaim, such as business entertainment.

- records of any goods exported.

- any adjustments, such as corrections to the accounts or amended VAT invoices.

Generally all business records that are relevant for VAT must be kept for at least six years. If this causes serious problems in terms of storage or costs, then HMRC may allow some records to be kept for a shorter period. Records may be stored digitally especially if that is needed to overcome storage and access difficulties.

Keeping a VAT account

A VAT account is the separate record that must be kept of the VAT charged on taxable sales (referred to as output tax or VAT payable) and the VAT paid on purchases (called input tax or VAT reclaimable). It provides the link between the business records and the VAT Return. A VAT-registered business needs to add up the VAT in the sales and purchases records and then transfer these totals to the VAT account, using separate headings for VAT payable and VAT reclaimable.

The VAT account can be kept in whatever way suits the business best, as long as it includes information about the VAT that it:

- owes on sales, including when fuel scale charges are used
- owes on acquisitions from other European Union (EU) countries
- owes following a correction or error adjustment
- can reclaim on business purchases
- can reclaim on acquisitions from other EU countries
- can reclaim following a correction or error adjustment
- is reclaiming via VAT bad debt relief

The business must also keep records of any adjustments that have been made, such as balancing payments for the annual accounting scheme for VAT.

Information from the VAT account can be used to complete the VAT Return at the end of each accounting period. VAT reclaimable is subtracted from the VAT payable, to give the net amount of VAT to pay to or reclaim from HMRC.

Unless it is using the cash accounting scheme, a business:

- must pay the VAT charged on invoices to customers during the accounting period that relates to the return, even if those customers have not paid the invoices

- may reclaim the VAT charged on invoices from suppliers during the accounting period that relates to the return, even if it has not paid the invoices.

Exempt and partly-exempt businesses

Exempt goods and services

There are some goods and services on which VAT is not charged.

Exempt supplies are not taxable for VAT, so sales of exempt goods and services are not included in taxable turnover for VAT purposes. If a registered business buys exempt items, there is no VAT to reclaim.

This is different to zero-rated supplies. In both cases VAT is not added to the selling price, but zero-rated goods or services are taxable for VAT at 0%, and are included in taxable turnover.

Business which only sell or supply exempt goods or services

A business which only supplies goods or services that are exempt from VAT is called an exempt business. It cannot register for VAT, so it will not be able to reclaim any input tax on business purchases.

Again this is different to zero-rated supplies, as a business can reclaim the input tax on any purchases that relate to zero-rated sales. In addition, a business which sells mainly or only zero-rated items may apply for an exemption from VAT registration, but then it can't claim back any input tax.

Reclaiming VAT in a partly-exempt business

A business that is registered for VAT but that makes some exempt supplies is referred to as partly, or partially, exempt.

Generally, such businesses won't be able to reclaim the input tax paid on purchases that relate to exempt supplies.

However if the amount of input tax incurred relating to exempt supplies is below a minimum 'de minimus' amount, input tax can be reclaimed in full.

If the amount of input tax incurred relating to exempt supplies is above the 'de minimus' amount, only the part of the input tax that related to non-exempt supplies can be reclaimed.

Place of supply

Businesses which make supplies of goods and services to other member states of the EU or to countries outside the EU, or which receive goods and services from other member states of the EU or from countries outside the EU, must apply the "place of supply" rules for both goods and services. Place of supply is important because it drives the amount of VAT, if any, which is to be added to the cost of the services, and the manner in which any VAT is accounted for.

The place of supply is the place, or country, where the supply is made.

The following rules apply to a supplier based in the UK, with no alternative location elsewhere in the EU or outside the EU.

Supplies and receipts of goods

The place of supply for goods is always the country where the goods originate. This applies whether the goods are for the enjoyment of a business customer or a domestic customer.

Supplies and receipts of services

Supplies of services are covered by the "Place of supply of services order" or POSSO. Here the place of supply can be different depending on who the customer is, and whether the supply of services is within, or outside, the EU.

When the customer is a business customer the place of supply is where the customer is.

Should the customer be either:

* a non-business,
* an unregistered business, or
* a registered business, but the supply is of a non-business nature.

then the place of supply is the country where the supplier is, irrespective of where the customer is.

Tax points

The time of supply, known as the 'tax point', is the date when a transaction takes place for VAT purposes. This date is not necessarily the date the supply physically takes place.

Generally, a registered business must pay or reclaim VAT in the (usually quarterly) VAT period, or tax period, in which the time of supply occurs, and it must use the correct rate of VAT in force on that date. This means knowing the time of supply/tax point for every transaction is important, as it must be put on the right VAT Return.

Time of supply (tax point) for goods and services

The time of supply for VAT purposes is defined as follows:

- for transactions where no VAT invoice is issued, the time of supply is normally the date the supply takes place (as defined below).

- for transactions where there is a VAT invoice, the time of supply is normally the date the invoice is issued, even if this is after the date the supply took place (as defined below).

To issue a VAT invoice, it must be sent (by post, email etc.) or given to the customer for them to keep. A tax point cannot be created simply by preparing an invoice.

However there are exceptions to these rules on time of supply, detailed below.

Date the supply takes place

For goods, the time when the goods are considered to be supplied for VAT purposes is the date when one of the following happens.

- the supplier sends the goods to the customer.

- the customer collects the goods from the supplier.

- the goods (which are not either sent or collected) are made available for the customer to use, for example if the supplier is assembling something on the customer's premises.

For services, the date when the services are supplied for VAT purposes is the date when the service is carried out and all the work - except invoicing - is finished.

Exceptions regarding time of supply (tax point)

The above general principles for working out the time of supply do not apply in the following situations:

- for transactions where a VAT invoice is issued, or payment is received, in advance of the date of supply, the time of supply is the date the invoice is issued or the payment is received, whichever is the earlier.

- if the supplier receives full payment before the date when the supply takes place and no VAT invoice has yet been issued, the time of supply is the date the payment is received.

- if the supplier receives part-payment before the date when the supply takes place, the time of supply becomes the date the part-payment is received but only for the amount of the part-payment (assuming no VAT invoice has been issued before this date - in which case the time of supply is the date the invoice is issued). The time of supply for the remainder will follow the normal rules - and might fall in a different VAT period, and so have to go onto a different VAT Return.

- if the supplier issues a VAT invoice more than 14 days after the date when the supply took place, the time of supply will be the date the supply took place, and not the date the invoice is issued. However, if a supplier has genuine commercial difficulties in invoicing within 14 days of the supply taking place, they can contact HMRC to ask for permission to issue invoices later than 14 days and move the time of supply to this later date.

- where services are being supplied on a continuous basis over a period in excess of a month but invoices are being issued regularly throughout the period. A tax point is created every time an invoice is issued or a payment is made, whichever happens first. A business may issue invoices for a whole 12 month period but only if it is known that payments will be made regularly.

- goods supplied to a customer on a sale or return basis remain the property of the supplier until the customer indicates they are intending to keep them. If a time limit has been fixed for the sale or return the tax point is:

  - where the fixed period is 12 months or less – the date the time limit expires

  - where the fixed period is more than 12 months, or there is no fixed period – 12 months from the date the goods were sent

  - where the customer adopts the goods before the fixed period has expired – the date the goods are adopted.

A payment made, which is not returnable, normally indicates that the goods have been adopted, however the receipt of a deposit which is repayable if the goods are returned is not an indication of adoption.

VAT invoices

To whom is a VAT invoice is issued?

Whenever a VAT-registered business supplies taxable goods or services to another VAT-registered business, it must give the customer a VAT invoice.

A VAT-registered business is not required to issue a VAT invoice to a non-registered business or to a member of the public, but it must do so if requested.

What is a VAT invoice?

A VAT invoice shows certain VAT details of a supply of goods or services. It can be either in paper or electronic form. An electronic invoice (e-invoice) is only valid if it is in a secure format, for example a "pdf".

A VAT-registered customer must have a valid VAT invoice from the supplier in order to claim back the VAT they have paid on the purchase for their business.

What is not a VAT invoice?

The following are NOT VAT invoices:

- pro-forma invoices
- invoices for only zero-rated or exempt supplies
- invoices that state 'this is not a VAT invoice'
- statements of account
- delivery notes
- orders
- letters, emails or other correspondence.

A registered business cannot reclaim the VAT it has paid on a purchase by using these documents as proof of payment.

What a VAT invoice must show

A VAT invoice must show:

- an invoice number which is unique and follows on from the number of the previous invoice - any spoiled or cancelled serially numbered invoice must be kept to show to a VAT officer at the next VAT inspection

- the seller's name or trading name, and address

- the seller's VAT registration number

- the invoice date

- the time of supply or tax point if this is different from the invoice date

- the customer's name or trading name, and address

- a description sufficient to identify the goods or services supplied to the customer.

For each different type of item listed on the invoice, the business must show:

- the unit price or rate, excluding VAT
- the quantity of goods or the extent of the services
- the rate of VAT that applies to what is being sold
- the total amount payable, excluding VAT
- the rate of any cash or settlement discount
- the total amount of VAT charged.

If the business issues a VAT invoice that includes zero-rated or exempt goods or services, it must:

- show clearly that there is no VAT payable on those goods or services
- show the total of those values separately.

Where a prompt payment discount (PPD) is offered VAT must be accounted for to HMRC on the actual consideration received. The business must decide how to express this on the invoice. It may:

- invoice at the discounted value with VAT on that amount and then issue an additional invoice for the discount plus VAT at the point it becomes clear the customer will not take the discount by paying within the prompt payment period, or

- invoice for the full value with VAT on that amount and then issue a credit note for the discount plus VAT should the customer pay the discounted value within the prompt payment period, or

- invoice for the full value of the supply and associated VAT but provide information to the customer which allows it to determine how much to pay if they make payment within the prompt payment discount period. This information must include details of the input tax which they are permitted to recover depending on when they make payment. A warning should be included to the customer that failure to account for the correct amount of VAT is an offence.

Rounding on VAT invoices

The total VAT payable on all goods and services shown on a VAT invoice may be rounded down to a whole penny. Any fraction of a penny can be ignored. (This concession is not available to retailers.)

Time limits for issuing VAT invoices

There is a strict time limit on issuing VAT invoices. Normally a VAT invoice to a VAT-registered customer must be issued within 30 days of the basic tax point, which is either the date of supply of the goods or services, subject to the 14 day rule or, if the business was paid in advance, the date payment was received. This is so the customer can claim back the VAT on the supply, if they are entitled to do so.

The 30 day limit for goods starts with the day the goods are sent to the customer or taken by the customer or made available to the customer.

Invoices cannot be issued any later without permission from HMRC, except in a few limited circumstances.

A valid VAT invoice is needed to reclaim VAT

Even if a business is registered for VAT, it can normally only reclaim VAT on purchases if:

- they are for use in the business or for business purposes and
- a valid VAT invoice for the purchase is received and retained*.

*Subject to the rules for VAT invoices for supplies of £250 or less including VAT and for supplies of £25 including VAT or less:

- a simplified invoice for supplies of £250 or less is acceptable as a "valid VAT invoice" for input tax reclaim.

- supplies of £25 or less including VAT, supported by a simple till receipt, can be assumed to be acceptable as a "valid VAT invoice" for input tax reclaim as long as the business has a reasonable understanding that the supplier is VAT registered.

Only VAT-registered businesses can issue valid VAT invoices. A business cannot reclaim VAT on any goods or services that are purchased from a business that is not VAT-registered.

Where simplified (less detailed) VAT invoices can be issued

Simplified VAT invoices

If a VAT-registered business makes taxable supplies of goods or services for £250 or less including VAT, then it can issue a simplified (less detailed) VAT invoice that only needs to show:

- the seller's name and address
- the seller's VAT registration number
- the time of supply (tax point)
- a description of the goods or services
- the total payable including VAT.

If the supply includes items at different VAT rates then, for each different VAT rate, the simplified VAT invoice must also show the VAT rate applicable to the item(s).

There is no requirement for the business making the supply to keep copies of any less detailed invoices it has issued.

Pro-forma invoices

If there is a need to issue a sales document for goods or services not supplied yet, the business can issue a 'pro-forma' invoice or a similar document as part of the offer to supply goods or services to customers.

A pro-forma invoice is not a VAT invoice, and it should be clearly marked with the words "This is not a VAT invoice".

If a potential customer accepts the goods or services offered to them and these are actually supplied, then a VAT invoice must be issued within the appropriate time limit if appropriate.

If the business has been issued with a pro-forma invoice by a supplier it cannot be used to claim back VAT on the purchase. A VAT invoice must be obtained from the supplier.

Advanced payments or deposits

An advance payment, or deposit, is a proportion of the total selling price that a customer pays before they are supplied with goods or services. When a business asks for an advance payment or deposit, the tax point is whichever of the following happens first:

- the date a VAT invoice is issued for the advance payment
- the date the advance payment is received

The business must include the VAT on the advance payment or deposit on the VAT Return for the period when the tax point occurs.

If the customer pays any remaining balance before the goods are delivered or the services are performed, another tax point is created when whichever of the following happens first:

- a VAT invoice is issued for the balance
- payment of the balance is received.

The VAT on the balance must be included on the VAT Return for the period when the tax point occurs.

VAT does not have to be accounted for if a deposit is either:

- refunded to the customer in full when they return goods safely, or
- kept as compensation for loss of or damage to the goods.

Discounts on good and services

If any goods or services supplied by a VAT-registered business are subject to a trade, bulk or other form of discount, VAT is charged on the VAT invoice on the discounted price rather than the full price.

Returned goods, credit notes, bad debts and VAT

For a buyer who has received a VAT invoice

If goods are returned to the seller for full or partial credit there are three options:

- return the invoice to the supplier and obtain a replacement invoice showing the proper amount of VAT due, if any
- obtain a credit note from the supplier
- issue a debit note to the supplier.

If the buyer issues a debit note or receives a credit note, it must:

- record this in the accounting records

- enter it on the next VAT Return, deducting the VAT on the credit or debit note from the amount of VAT which can be reclaimed.

For a seller who has issued a VAT invoice

If goods are returned by a customer, there are again three options:

1. cancel and recover the original invoice, and issue a replacement showing the correct amount of any VAT due, if any

2. issue a credit note to the customer

3. obtain a debit note from the customer.

If the seller issues a credit note or receives a debit note, it must:

- record this in the accounting records

- enter it on the next VAT Return, deducting the VAT on the credit or debit note from the amount of VAT payable.

Entertainment expenses

Business entertainment

Business entertainment is any form of free or subsidised entertainment or hospitality to non-employees, for example suppliers and customers. Generally a business cannot reclaim input tax on business entertainment expenses. The exception is that input tax can be reclaimed in respect of entertaining overseas customers, but not UK or Isle of Man customers.

Employee expenses and entertainment

The business can, however, reclaim VAT on employee expenses and employee entertainment expenses if those expenses relate to travel and subsistence or where the entertainment applies only to employees.

When the entertainment is in respect of a mixed group of both employees and non-employees (e.g. customers and/or suppliers), the business can only reclaim VAT on the proportion of the expenses that is for employees and on the proportion for overseas customers.

Vehicles and motoring expenses

VAT and vehicles

When it buys a car a registered business generally cannot reclaim the VAT. There are some exceptions - for example, when the car is used mainly as one of the following:

- a taxi
- for driving instruction
- for self-drive hire.

If the VAT on the original purchase price of a car bought new is not reclaimed, the business does not have to charge any VAT when it is sold. This is because the sale of the car is exempt for VAT purposes. If the business did reclaim the VAT when it bought the car new, VAT is chargeable when it comes to sell it.

VAT-registered businesses can generally reclaim the VAT when they buy a commercial vehicle such as a van, lorry or tractor.

Reclaiming VAT on road fuel

- If the business pays for road fuel, it can deal with the VAT charged on the fuel in one of four ways:

- reclaim all of the VAT. All of the fuel must be used only for business purposes.

- reclaim all of the VAT and pay the appropriate fuel scale charge - this is a way of accounting for output tax on fuel that the business buys but that is then used for private motoring.

- reclaim only the VAT that relates to fuel used for business mileage. Detailed records of business and private mileage must be kept.

- do not reclaim any VAT. This can be a useful option if mileage is low and also if fuel is used for both business and private motoring. If the business chooses this option it must apply it to all vehicles, including commercial vehicles.

Transactions outside the UK

Exports, despatches and supplying goods abroad: charging VAT

If a business sells, supplies or transfers goods out of the UK to someone in another country it may need to charge VAT on them.

VAT on exports of goods to non-EU countries

Generally speaking, the business can zero-rate supplies exported outside the EU, provided it follows strict rules, obtains and keeps the necessary evidence, and obeys all laws.

The term 'exports' is reserved to describe sales to a country outside the EU. Goods supplied to another EU member state are technically known as despatches rather than exports.

VAT on despatches of goods to someone who is not VAT registered in another EU member state

When a business supplies goods to someone in another EU member state, and they are not registered for VAT in that country, it should normally charge VAT*.

VAT on despatches of goods to someone who is VAT registered in another EU member state

*If, however, goods are supplied to someone who is registered for VAT in the destination EU member state, the business can zero-rate the supply for VAT purposes, provided it meets certain conditions.

Imports, acquisitions and purchasing goods from abroad: paying and reclaiming VAT

Generally speaking, VAT is payable on all purchases of goods that are bought from abroad at the same rate that would apply to the goods if bought in the UK. The business must tell HMRC about goods that it imports, and pay any VAT and duty that is due.

VAT on imports of goods from non-EU countries

VAT may be charged on imports of goods bought from non-EU countries. The business can reclaim any VAT paid on the goods imported as input tax.

VAT on goods acquired from EU member states

If a business is registered for VAT in the UK and buys goods from inside the EU, these are known as acquisitions rather than imports. Usually no VAT is charged by the supplier but acquisition tax, at the same rate of VAT that would apply if the goods were supplied in the UK, is due on the acquisition. This is included in Box 2 of the VAT return. It can be reclaimed as input tax in Box 4 of the VAT return as if the goods were bought in the UK.

Bad debts

When a business can reclaim VAT on bad debts

VAT that has been paid to HMRC and which has not been received from the customer can be reclaimed as bad debt relief. The conditions are that:

- the debt is more than six months and less than four years and six months old
- the debt has been written off in the VAT account and transferred to a separate bad debt account
- the debt has not been sold or handed to a factoring company
- the business did not charge more than the normal selling price for the items.

Bad debt relief does not apply when the cash accounting scheme is used because the VAT is not paid to HMRC until after the customer has paid it to the supplier.

How to claim bad debt relief

If the business is entitled to claim bad debt relief, add the amount of VAT to be reclaimed to the amount of VAT being reclaimed on purchases (input tax) and put the total figure in Box 4 of the VAT Return.

Effect of a change in the business

If a business closes down, relief for all outstanding bad debts up to and including the date of closure will need to be claimed, if eligible.

Where a business is acquired as a going concern and the acquiring business takes on the VAT registration of the closing business, it may be possible to transfer the outstanding bad debts from the old to the new business.

Completing the online VAT Return, box by box

The online VAT Return is completed as follows.

Box 1 – VAT due in this period on sales and other outputs:

- this is the total amount of VAT charged on sales to customers. It also has to include VAT due to HMRC for other reasons, for example fuel scale charges.

- include VAT due on a supply of services from another member state of the EC, where the supplier has "zero-rated" the supply.

Box 2 – VAT due in this period on acquisitions from other EC Member States:

- VAT due, but not yet paid, on goods bought from other EU member states, and any services directly related to those goods (such as delivery charges). The business may be able to reclaim this amount, and if so it must be included in the total in Box 4.

Box 3 – Total VAT due (the sum of boxes 1 and 2). This is calculated automatically by the online return.

Box 4 – VAT reclaimed in this period on purchases and other inputs (including acquisitions from the EC):

- this is the VAT charged on purchases for use in the business. It should also include:

- VAT paid on imports from countries outside the EC

- VAT due (but not yet paid) on goods from other EC member states, and any services directly related to those goods (such as delivery charges) - this is the figure in Box 2.

- VAT due on a supply of services from a supplier in another member state of the EC where that supply has been "zero-rated" by the supplier. This will be the same amount as entered in Box 1 in respect of the same transaction.

Box 5 – Net VAT to be paid to HM Revenue & Customs or reclaimed by you (Difference between boxes 3 and 4). This is calculated automatically by the online return.

Box 6 – Total value of sales and all other outputs excluding any VAT. Include your box 8 figure:

- enter the total figure for sales (excluding VAT) for the period, that is the sales on which the VAT entered in Box 1 was based. Additionally, also include:

- any zero-rated and exempt sales or other supplies made

- any amount entered in Box 8

- exports to outside the EC.

The net amount of any credit notes issued, or debit notes received, is deducted.

Box 7 – Total value of purchases and all other inputs excluding any VAT. Include your box 9 figure:

- enter the total figure for purchases (excluding VAT) for the period, that is the purchases on which the VAT entered in Box 4 was based. Additionally, also include:

- any zero-rated and exempt purchases

- any amount entered in Box 9

- imports from outside the EU.

Box 8 – Total value of all supplies of goods and related costs, excluding any VAT, to other EC Member States:

- enter the total value of goods supplied to another EC member state and services related to those goods (such as delivery charges).

Box 9 – Total value of all acquisitions of goods and related costs, excluding any VAT, from other EC Member States.

- enter the total value of goods received from VAT registered suppliers in another EC member state and services related to those goods (such as delivery charges).

VAT periods, submitting returns and paying VAT

VAT Returns for transactions to the end of the relevant VAT period must be submitted by the due date shown on the VAT Return. VAT due must also be paid by the due date.

What is a VAT period?

A VAT period is the period of time over which the business records VAT transactions in the VAT account for completion of the VAT Return. The VAT period is three months (a quarter) unless the annual accounting scheme is used. The end dates of a business's four VAT periods are determined when it first registers for VAT, but it can choose to amend the dates on which its VAT periods end. This is often done to match VAT periods to accounting period ends.

Submitting VAT Returns online and paying HMRC electronically

It is mandatory for virtually all VAT-registered traders to submit their VAT Returns to HMRC using online filing, and to pay HMRC electronically.

Submitting Vat Returns – Making Tax Digital (MTD)

VAT-registered businesses with a taxable turnover above the VAT threshold are required to use the MTD service to keep records digitally and use software to submit their VAT returns for VAT periods starting on, or after, 1 April 2019. The exception to this is a small minority of VAT-registered businesses with more complex requirements.

Under MTD the software which businesses use must be capable of keeping and maintaining records, preparing their VAT Returns, and communicating with HMRC digitally via their Application Programming Interface (API) platform.

If a business is required to register for MTD as a result of having taxable turnover above the registration threshold, it must continue to keep digital records and submit its returns digitally even if it falls below the VAT registration threshold at a future point in time. This obligation does not apply if the business deregisters from VAT or meets other exemption criteria.

If a business is exempt from MTD because taxable turnover is below the VAT registration threshold it may still choose to follow the Making Tax Digital rules. The business must notify HMRC in writing before the start of the VAT period in which it wishes to start using MTD. If a business has started using MTD voluntarily, and later decides it no longer wishes to follow the MTD rules, it must notify HMRC in writing and will no longer be required to follow the MTD rules from the start of the next VAT period after notification to HMRC.

A business will not have to follow the rules for MTD if HMRC is satisfied that either:

- it is not reasonably practicable for the business to use digital tools to keep business records or submit VAT Returns because of age, disability, remoteness of location or for any other reason

- the business is subject to an insolvency procedure

- the business is run entirely by practising members of a religious society or order whose beliefs are incompatible with using electronic communications or keeping electronic records.

HMRC have allowed a one year period until 1 April 2020, known as the "soft landing period", for businesses to have in place digital links between all parts of their functional compatible software.

A 'digital link' is one where a transfer or exchange of data is made, or can be made, electronically between software programs, products or applications, without the involvement or need for manual intervention such as the copying over of information by hand or the manual transposition of data between two or more pieces of software.

During the soft landing period only, where a digital link has not been established between software programs, HMRC will accept the use of 'cut and paste' or 'copy and paste' as being a digital link for these VAT periods.

The submission of information to HMRC must always be via an Application Programming Interface (API). While HMRC expects most businesses to use API-enabled commercial software packages both to keep digital records and file their VAT Returns, bridging software or API-enabled spreadsheets may be used as an alternative.

Due dates for submitting the VAT Return and paying electronically

Businesses are responsible for calculating how much VAT they owe and for paying VAT so that the amount clears to HMRC's bank account on or before the due date. Paying on time avoids having to pay a surcharge for late payment.

The normal due date for submitting each VAT Return and electronically paying HMRC any VAT that is owed is one calendar month after the end of the relevant VAT period, unless the annual accounting scheme is operated. The normal due date for the return and payment can be found on the return.

Online filing and electronic payment mean that businesses get an extended due date for filing the return of seven extra calendar days after the normal due date shown on the VAT Return. This extra seven days also applies to paying HMRC so that the amount has cleared into HMRC's bank account. However this does not apply if the business uses the Annual Accounting Scheme for VAT.

If the business pays HMRC by Direct Debit, HMRC automatically collects payment from the business's bank account three bank working days after the extra seven calendar days following the normal due date.

If the business fails to pay cleared funds into HMRC's bank account by the payment deadline, or fails to have sufficient funds in its account to meet the direct debit, it may be liable to a surcharge for late payment.

Repayment of VAT

If the amount of VAT reclaimed (entered in Box 4) is more than the VAT to be paid (entered in Box 3), then the net VAT value in Box 5 is a repayment due to the business from HMRC.

HMRC is obliged to schedule this sum for repayment automatically, provided checks applied to the VAT Return do not indicate that such a repayment might not be due. There may be circumstances when the business does not receive the repayment automatically, for instance if there is an outstanding debt owed to HMRC.

Special accounting schemes

Annual Accounting Scheme for VAT

Using standard VAT accounting, four VAT Returns each year are required. Any VAT due is payable quarterly, and any VAT refunds due are also receivable quarterly.

Using the normal annual accounting scheme, the business makes nine interim payments at monthly intervals. There is only one VAT Return to complete, at the end of the year, when either a balancing payment is payable or a balancing refund is receivable.

Businesses can start on the annual accounting scheme if their estimated taxable turnover during the next tax year is not more than £1.35 million. Businesses already using the annual accounting scheme can continue to do so until the estimated taxable turnover for the next tax year exceeds £1.6 million. If the business is taken over as a going concern the acquiring business must assess the use of the annual accounting scheme in the context of the expected and combined turnover of the new business, and must immediately cease using the scheme if that is expected to exceed £1.6m.

Whilst using the annual accounting scheme the business may also be able to use either the cash accounting scheme or the flat rate scheme, but not both.

Benefits of annual accounting

- one VAT Return per year, instead of four.

- two months after the tax period end to complete and send in the annual VAT Return and pay the balance of VAT payable, rather than the usual one month.

- better management of cash flow by paying a fixed amount in nine instalments.

- ability to make additional payments as and when required.

- join from VAT registration day, or at any other time if already registered for VAT.

Disadvantages of annual accounting

- only one repayment per year, which is not beneficial if the business regularly requires refunds.

- if turnover decreases, interim payments may be higher than the VAT payments would be under standard VAT accounting – again there is a need to wait until the end of the year to receive a refund.

Cash Accounting Scheme for VAT

Using standard VAT accounting, VAT is paid on sales within a VAT period whether or not the customer has paid. VAT is reclaimed on purchases whether or not the business has paid the supplier.

Using cash accounting, VAT is not paid until the customer has paid the invoice. If a customer never pays, the business never has to pay the VAT. VAT is reclaimed on purchases only when the business has paid the invoice.

Cash accounting can be used if the estimated taxable turnover during the next tax year is not more than £1.35 million. A business can continue to use cash accounting until its taxable turnover exceeds £1.6 million.

The cash accounting scheme may be used in conjunction with the annual accounting scheme but not with the flat rate scheme. If the business is taken over as a going concern the acquiring business must assess the use of the cash accounting scheme in the context of the expected and combined turnover of the new business, and must immediately cease using the scheme if that is expected to exceed £1.6m.

Benefits of cash accounting

Using cash accounting may help cash flow, especially if customers are slow payers. Payment of VAT is not made until the business has received payment from the customer, so if a customer never pays, VAT does not have to be paid on that bad debt as long as the business is using the cash accounting scheme.

Disadvantages of cash accounting

Using cash accounting may adversely affect cash flow:

- the business cannot reclaim VAT on purchases until it has paid for them. This can be a disadvantage if most goods and services are purchased on credit.

- businesses which regularly reclaim more VAT than they pay will usually receive repayment later under cash accounting than under standard VAT accounting, unless they pay for everything at the time of purchase.

- if a business starts using cash accounting when it starts trading, it will not be able to reclaim VAT on most start-up expenditure, such as initial stock, tools or machinery, until it has actually paid for those items.

- when it leaves the cash accounting scheme the business will have to account for all outstanding VAT due, including on any bad debts.

Flat Rate Scheme for VAT

If its VAT-exclusive taxable turnover is less than £150,000 per year, the business could simplify its VAT accounting by registering on the Flat Rate Scheme and calculating VAT payments as a percentage of its total VAT-inclusive turnover. There is no reclaim of VAT on purchases - this is taken into account in calculating the flat rate percentage that applies to the business.

The VAT flat rate the business uses usually depends on its business type. It may pay a different rate if it only spends a small amount on goods.

Limited cost business

The business is classed as a 'limited cost business' if its goods cost less than either:

- 2% of its turnover
- £1,000 a year (if its costs are more than 2%).

This means the business pays a flat rate of 16.5%, whatever its business type.

Non-limited cost businesses use their business type to determine the applicable flat rate.

Reclaim of VAT on capital expenditure goods

If the business uses the Flat Rate Scheme, it can reclaim the VAT it has been charged on a single purchase of capital expenditure goods where the amount of the purchase, including VAT, is £2,000 or more. These capital expenditure goods are dealt with outside the Flat Rate Scheme. This means that the input tax is claimed in box 4 of the VAT return. If the supply is:

- more than one purchase
- under £2,000 including VAT, or
- of services.

Then no VAT is claimable, as this input tax is already taken into account in the calculation of the flat rate percentage.

The flat rate scheme can reduce the time needed in accounting for and working out VAT. Even though the business still needs to show a VAT amount on each VAT invoice issued, it does not need to record how much VAT it charged on every sale in its ledger accounts. Nor does it need to record the VAT paid on every purchase.

Once on the scheme, the business can continue to use it until its total business income exceeds £230,000. If the business is taken over as a going concern the acquiring business must assess the use of the flat rate scheme in the context of the expected and combined turnover of the new business, and must immediately cease using the scheme if that is expected to exceed £230,000. The flat rate scheme may be used in conjunction with the annual accounting scheme but not the cash accounting scheme.

Benefits of using the flat rate scheme

Using the flat rate scheme can save time and smooth cash flow. It offers these benefits:

- no need to record the VAT charged on every sale and purchase, as with standard VAT accounting. This can save time. But although the business only has to pay HMRC a percentage of its turnover, it must still show VAT at the appropriate normal rate (standard, reduced or zero) on the VAT invoices it issues.

- a first year discount. A business in its first year of VAT registration gets a 1% reduction in the applicable flat rate percentage until the day before the first anniversary of VAT registration.

- fewer rules to follow, for instance no longer having to work out what VAT on purchases can or cannot be reclaimed.

- peace of mind, less chance of mistakes and fewer worries about getting the VAT right.

- certainty. The business always knows what percentage of takings has to be paid to HMRC.

Potential disadvantages of using the flat rate scheme

The flat rate percentages are calculated in a way that takes into account zero-rated and exempt sales. They also contain an allowance for the VAT spent on purchases. So the VAT Flat Rate Scheme might not be right for the business if:

- it buys mostly standard-rated items, as there is no reclaim of any VAT on purchases

- it regularly receives a VAT repayment under standard VAT accounting

- it makes a lot of zero-rated or exempt sales.

- It is a 'limited cost business'.

Errors in previous VAT Returns

Action to be taken at the end of the VAT period

At the end of the VAT period, the business should calculate the net value of all the errors and omissions found during the period that relate to VAT Returns already submitted - that is, any tax which should have been claimed back is subtracted from any additional tax due to HMRC, and any tax that should have been paid is added. Any deliberate errors must not be included - these must be separately declared to HMRC.

What the business should do next depends on whether the net value of all the errors is less than or greater than the 'error correction reporting threshold', which is the greater of:

- £10,000

- 1% of the box 6 figure on the VAT Return for the period when the error was discovered - subject to an upper limit of £50,000

If the net value of all the errors is less than the error reporting threshold then, if preferred, the errors may be corrected by making an adjustment on the current VAT Return (Method 1).

However, if the value of the net VAT error discovered is above this threshold, it must be declared to HMRC separately, in writing (Method 2).

How to adjust the VAT Return: Method 1

Errors from previous VAT Returns can be corrected by adjusting the VAT amounts on the current VAT Return.

At the end of the VAT period when the errors are discovered, the VAT account of output tax due or input tax claimed is adjusted by the net amount of all errors. The VAT account must show the amount of the adjustment being made to the VAT Return.

If more than one error is discovered in the same exercise, the net value of all the errors is used to adjust the VAT liability on the VAT Return.

Either Box 1 or Box 4 is adjusted, as appropriate. For example, if the business discovers that it did not account for VAT payable to HMRC of £100 on a supply made in the past, and also did not account for £60 VAT reclaimable on a purchase, it should add £40 to the Box 1 figure on the current VAT Return.

How to separately declare an error to HMRC: Method 2

For certain errors a separate declaration is required to the relevant HMRC VAT Error Correction Team in writing about the mistake. The simplest way to tell them is to use Form VAT 652 "Notification of Errors in VAT Returns", which is for reporting errors on previous returns, but the business does not have to use Form VAT 652 - it can simply write a letter instead.

Businesses may, if they wish, use this method for errors of any size, even those which are below the error reporting threshold i.e. instead of a Method 1 error correction. Using this method means the business must not make adjustment for the same errors on a later VAT Return.

Method 2 must always be used if the net error exceeds the error reporting threshold or if the errors made on previous returns were made deliberately.

Surcharges, penalties and assessments

Surcharges for missed VAT Return or VAT payment deadlines

VAT-registered businesses must submit a VAT Return and pay any VAT by the relevant due date. If HMRC receives a return or VAT payment after the due date, the business is 'in default' and may have to pay a surcharge in addition to the VAT that is owed.

The first default is dealt with by a warning known as a 'Surcharge Liability Notice'. This notice tells the business that if it submits or pays late ('defaults') again during the following 12 months - known as the surcharge period - it may be charged a surcharge.

Submitting or paying late again during the surcharge period could result in a 'default surcharge'. This is a percentage of any unpaid VAT owed. Where a correct return is not submitted at all, HMRC will estimate the amount of VAT owed and base the surcharge on that amount (this is known as an assessment – see below).

HMRC assessments

Businesses have a legal obligation to submit VAT Returns and pay any VAT owed to HMRC by the relevant due date. If they do not submit a return, HMRC can issue an assessment which shows the amount of VAT that HMRC believes it is owed, based on HMRC's best estimate.

Penalties for careless and deliberate errors

Careless and deliberate errors will be liable to a penalty, whether they are adjusted on the VAT Return or separately declared.

If a business discovers an error which is neither careless nor deliberate, HMRC expects that it will take steps to adjust or declare it, as appropriate. If the business fails to take such steps, the inaccuracy will be treated as careless and a penalty will be due.

Penalties for inaccurate returns

Penalties may be applied if a VAT Return is inaccurate, and correcting this means tax is unpaid, understated, over-claimed or under-assessed. Telling HMRC about inaccuracies as soon as the business is aware of them may reduce any penalty that is due, in some cases to zero.

Penalty for late registration

Failure to register for VAT with HMRC at the right time may make a business liable to a late registration penalty.

Penalty for failure to disclose business changes

A business which undergoes a change which either cancels the existing registration or otherwise alters the registration details will face a civil penalty if it fails to disclose the changes to HMRC within 30 days of the change.

Finding out more information about VAT

Most questions can be answered by referring to the VAT section of the HMRC website.

VAT Enquiries Helpline

If the answer to a question is not on the HMRC website, the quickest and easiest way is to ring the VAT Enquiries Helpline where most VAT questions can be answered.

Letters to HMRC

The VAT General Enquiries helpline can answer most questions relating to VAT, but there may be times when it is more appropriate to write to HMRC.

This would apply if:

*   the VAT information published by HMRC - either on the website or in printed notices and information sheets - has not answered a question

*   the VAT General Enquiries helpline has advised the business to write

*   there is real doubt about how VAT affects a particular transaction, personal situation or business.

If HMRC already publishes information that answers the question, their response will give the relevant details.

Visits by VAT officers

On a control visit to a business a VAT officer can examine VAT records to make sure that they are up to date. They also check that amounts claimed from or paid to the government are correct.

Index

14-day rule, 49

A
Acquisitions, 33, 37
Actual tax point, 49, 54
Annual accounting scheme, 86, 91
Assessments, 101

B
Bad debt relief, 52, 54, 61
Basic tax point, 49, 54
Books of prime entry, 62

C
Cars, 28
Cash accounting scheme, 85, 91
Cash and petty cash payments book, 54
Cash receipts book, 54
Change to VAT rate, 102
Control visits, 101
Credit notes, 48

D
Debit notes, 48
Deposits, 51
Deregistration, 17
Despatches, 33, 37
Discounts, 47

E
Entertaining, 28
Error correction reporting threshold, 107
Errors, 98
Evasion of VAT, 101, 107
Exempt supplies, 11, 19
Exports, 34, 37

F
Flat rate scheme, 88, 91
Fuel scale charge, 29, 37
Fundamental principles, 104
Future test, 12

H
Historic test, 12
HMRC website, 107
How to complete the VAT return, 68

I
Imports, 34, 37
Input VAT, 3
Input VAT or input tax, 7
Irrecoverable input VAT, 27
Irrecoverable VAT, 60

M
Making Tax Digital, 73

O
Output VAT, 3
Output VAT or output tax, 7

P
Partially exempt traders, 30, 37
Payment, 73
Penalties, 100
Place of supply, 33
Proforma invoice, 47, 54
Purchases day book, 54
Purchases returns day book, 54

R
Records, 44
Reduced-rated, 11
Registration, 12, 19
Rounding, 26

S

Sales day book, 54
Sales returns day book, 54
Settlement discounts, 47
Simplified invoice, 46, 54
Standard scheme, 85
Standard-rated, **11**
Standard-rated supplies, 19
Submission deadlines, 73
Surcharge liability notice, 100, 107

T

Tax point, 49, 54
Taxable person, 11
Taxable supplies, **11**

Taxable turnover, 13, 19
Trade discounts, 47

V

VAT account, 75
VAT control account, 59
VAT invoice, 45, 54
VAT period, 62
VAT return, 64, 75
Voluntary registration, 16

Z

Zero-rated, **11**
Zero-rated supplies, 19

REVIEW FORM

How have you used this Course Book?
(Tick one box only)

☐ Self study

☐ On a course_____

☐ Other _____

Why did you decide to purchase this Course Book? *(Tick one box only)*

☐ Have used BPP materials in the past

☐ Recommendation by friend/colleague

☐ Recommendation by a college lecturer

☐ Saw advertising

☐ Other _____

During the past six months do you recall seeing/receiving either of the following?
(Tick as many boxes as are relevant)

☐ Our advertisement in Accounting Technician

☐ Our Publishing Catalogue

Which (if any) aspects of our advertising do you think are useful?
(Tick as many boxes as are relevant)

☐ Prices and publication dates of new editions

☐ Information on Course Book content

☐ Details of our free online offering

☐ None of the above

Your ratings, comments and suggestions would be appreciated on the following areas of this Course Book.

	Very useful	Useful	Not useful
Chapter overviews	☐	☐	☐
Introductory section	☐	☐	☐
Quality of explanations	☐	☐	☐
Illustrations	☐	☐	☐
Chapter activities	☐	☐	☐
Test your learning	☐	☐	☐
Keywords	☐	☐	☐

	Excellent	Good	Adequate	Poor
Overall opinion of this Course Book	☐	☐	☐	☐

Do you intend to continue using BPP Products?   ☐ Yes   ☐ No

The BPP author of this edition can be emailed at: learningmedia@bpp.com

REVIEW FORM (continued)

TELL US WHAT YOU THINK

Please note any further comments and suggestions/errors below